Taxes and Value

The Ongoing Research and Analysis Relating to the S Corporation Valuation Puzzle

Nancy J. Fannon
and
Keith F. Sellers

BVR
What It's Worth
1000 SW Broadway, Suite 1200, Portland, OR 97205
(503) 291-7963 • www.bvresources.com

BVR
What It's Worth

Printed in the United States of America.

Publisher: Sarah Andersen

Managing Editor: Janice Prescott

Chair and CEO: David Foster

President: Lucretia Lyons

Vice President of Sales: Lexie Gross

Customer Service Manager: Retta Dodge

ISBN: 978-1-62150-050-6

Library of Congress Control Number: 2015936423

Disclaimer

While this guide endeavors to present the reader with a comprehensive review of the academic literature relating to the effect of taxes on the cost of capital, and suggests how such research might apply to private-company valuations, it does not constitute U.S. federal tax advice and is not intended or written to be used, and cannot be used, for the purpose of avoiding penalties under the Internal Revenue Code. Each reader should endeavor to understand and interpret the research and apply it in the appraisal of pass-through entities as they determine it best fits the particular situation.

Table of Contents

About the Authors 4

Acknowledgments 5

Introduction 7

Chapter 1. The Importance of Matching the Cost of Capital With the Income Stream 9

Chapter 2. Introduction to the Concept of Implicit Taxes 15

Chapter 3. An Explanation of the Implications of Shareholder Taxes on the Corporate Cost of Capital 23

Chapter 4. Literature Review: Research on the Effect of Taxes Embedded in the Cost of Capital 29

Chapter 5. Impact of Prior Research on Private-Company Valuation 41

Chapter 6. Foundation for Cash Flow-Based Models 45

Chapter 7. Research Related to the Magnitude of Taxes Embedded in the Cost of Capital 53

Chapter 8. An Alternative Approach to the Valuation of Pass-Through Entities 57

Appendix A. Suggested Areas for Further Research 67

Appendix B. Evolution of Pass-Through Entity Valuation 71

Appendix C. Understanding the Basics of the Cost of Capital 77

Appendix D. C Corporation Versus S Corporation Transaction Pricing 87

Appendix E. Digests of Cases Addressing Pass-Through Entity Issues 97

Appendix F. Bibliography 145

Appendix G. Links to Selected Academic Research Papers 153

About the Authors

Nancy J. Fannon is the partner in charge of Litigation Services with Meyers, Harrison and Pia LLC. She is a nationally known author and expert in the area of economic damages and corporate valuation. With over 25 years of experience as a financial analyst, she frequently serves as an expert witness or a financial consultant in matters involving complex corporate litigation for public and private companies and testifies or consults on matters involving economic damages, unjust enrichment/disgorgement, post-acquisition disputes, shareholder disputes, and other damages analyses. She has written for numerous valuation and damages journals, has published three books related to valuation and damages, and has been a technical reviewer or contributing author to several others. Her most recent text, the third edition of *The Comprehensive Guide to Lost Profits and Other Commercial Damages,* was published in 2014. Nancy is a frequent national speaker, has served on the editorial boards of four of the major valuation and economic analysis industry organizations, and served as co-chair of a joint industry standard-setting board. In 2007, she was inducted into the AICPA's Hall of Fame, awarded for substantial contributions to the advancement of the business valuation profession.

Keith F. Sellers, DBA, is an associate professor in the School of Accountancy at the Daniels College of Business at the University of Denver. Prior to joining the School of Accountancy, he was a professor at the University of North Alabama's College of Business, where he was the LaGrange Eminent Scholar of Business Valuation. Keith is an experienced business valuation consultant and has performed more than 400 valuations for clients in the banking, construction, manufacturing, retail, and service sectors all across the country. He is also co-founder of a consulting and software development company that specializes in the valuation of employee stock options, warrants, convertible equity securities, and other derivative financial instruments. Prior to teaching at the University of North Alabama, Keith taught at Fort Lewis College and the Sam M. Walton College of Business at the University of Arkansas.

Acknowledgments

Our heartfelt thanks go out to the panel of technical reviewers, whose thoughtful insights and comments added enormously to this text. Their time and careful review helped make this a much better and more thorough resource, and we are grateful for their time and efforts.

Michael Crain, DBA, CPA, ABV, ASA, CFA, CFE
Principal
The Financial Valuation Group
Fort Lauderdale, Fla.

Aswath Damodaran, Ph.D.
Kerschner Family Chair in Finance Education
Leonard N. Stern School of Business
New York, N.Y.

David Dufendach, CPA, ABV, ASA, MBA
Partner, Forensic and Valuation Services
Grant Thornton LLP
Seattle, Wash.

Michael Gregory, ASA, CVA
Chief Manager
Michael Gregory Consulting LLC
Roseville, Minn.

Theodore Israel, CPA, ABV, CFF, CVA
Partner
Israel Frey Group, LLP
San Rafael, Calif.

Kenneth Pia, CPA, ABV, ASA, MCBA
Partner in Charge of Business Valuation Services
Meyers, Harrison and Pia
New Haven, Conn.

Robert Ricketts, Ph.D.
Frank M. Burke Chair in Taxation
Department Head - Accounting
Rawls College of Business, Texas Tech University
Lubbock, Texas

We would also like to thank and acknowledge our staff members who assisted in various aspects of this guide, including Janine Talbot and Cameron Scott.

Introduction

The publication of this guide has been seven years in the making, and it could not have happened without the help and guidance of many individuals and researchers along the way. However, the publication of the guide does not mean that this work is done. To the contrary, the reason it has taken this long is the continually evolving nature of research.

We expect and welcome the continuance of this work in an effort to move the valuation profession forward on this controversial issue. In this guide, we set forth the findings of decades of academic research on the impact of taxes on firm value. Relying on this research, we demonstrate that historical market returns impound the effects of shareholder taxes, and these returns can be adjusted to estimate a cost of capital appropriate for pass-through entity valuation. We hope and expect that others will consider this work and build upon it, as well as suggest areas for improvement and furtherance of the analysis. However, the discussion presented herein should move the valuation profession ahead of the hypotheses and largely unfounded presumptions that have heretofore framed the tax-affecting discussion, by providing substantive data and information to inform their calculations.

This work adds to the critical and ongoing controversy in the valuation profession relating to the relative value of pass-through entities in contrast to publicly traded C corporations that are subject to double taxation (and from which the return used to value private companies using the income approach is derived).

It is intuitive to many analysts and investors that a company that is perceived to have a lower tax burden would have greater value (such as the perception of the relative tax burden of an S corporation and its investors compared to the perception of the tax burden borne by a public C corporation and its investors). However, it is the evidence and research that should guide our analysis—not our perception. The now infamous *Gross*[1] case (discussed in Appendix E) stated: "If … the discount rate is assumed to be an after-shareholder-tax rate of return, *then the cash-flow should be reduced ('tax affected') to an after-shareholder-tax amount.*" (emphasis added).

As of the writing of this guide, *no court has been presented evidence* that demonstrates that the discount rate *is* affected by shareholder taxes. It is that evidence which this book seeks to address, by presenting the evidence of the effect of taxes on value. We then suggest how analysts might consider this evidence in their valuation of closely held businesses.

1 *Gross v. Commissioner*, T.C. Memo 1999-254, aff'd, 272 F.3d 333 F.3d (6th Cir. 2001)

We begin our analysis in Chapter 1 with an overview of the concept of matching the cost of capital with the income stream. The terminology analysts use to talk about the cost of capital has caused a great deal of confusion about how taxes affect it and the appropriate income stream to apply it to. Chapter 1 seeks to address this issue. Chapters 2 and 3 present an explanation of the concept of explicit taxes and an explanation of how taxes affect value. These chapters are precursors for Chapters 4 and 5, which present a literature review of research related to the impact of taxes on value and the implications of it for private-company valuation. Chapter 6 presents a summary of prior methods used by valuation analysts. We then review the literature related to the magnitude of tax effects on value in Chapter 7 and conclude in Chapter 8 with suggestions for how the research might impact the manner in which analysts value pass-through entities.

Readers looking to this guide for a "quick fix" to the issue of how to value a pass-through entity will be disappointed: There are no easy answers, and the research is both dense and has further to go; our suggestions for areas of further research can be found in Appendix A. However, as outlined in this Guide, the breadth and depth of information currently available allows us to make informed inferences and arrive at reasonable valuation conclusions—just as we do in nearly every aspect of private-company valuation.

Our analysis presumes that the reader has a basic understanding of the evolution of this issue in the business valuation profession and in the courts. It also assumes that the reader has a firm understanding of how the cost of capital that most private-company analysts use is developed. These topics are important precedents to understanding the research and analysis presented herein. For readers seeking more information on these subjects, please refer to Appendix B ("The Evolution of Pass-Through Entity Valuation"), Appendix C ("Understanding the Basics of the Cost of Capital"), and Appendix E ("Abstracts of Cases Addressing Pass-Through Entity Valuation"). Additionally, studies of transactions of C versus S corporations have provided insight into the existence and magnitude of pricing differentials. A summary of these studies, as well as our own study, can be found in Appendix D.

For the reader desiring a more in-depth understanding of the academic literature, Appendix F provides our complete bibliography of resources and Appendix G provides links to some of the most relevant research papers.

We hope that the research and analysis in this guide will assist the profession in moving its long-struggling quest to solve the pass-through entity valuation puzzle forward.

Nancy Fannon and Keith F. Sellers
2015

Chapter 1. The Importance of Matching the Cost of Capital With the Income Stream

Most analysts value S corporations[1] at least in part by employing the income approach. The models used in several Tax Court decisions, and the models used by most valuation analysts (both of which are discussed later in this text), incorporate certain underlying assumptions about the effect of taxes in the public market (from which we derive our cost of capital). It is *these underlying assumptions* related to income approach models for valuing S corporations that this text will identify and address.[2]

The two components required to value an S corporation using an income approach are: a metric of the S corporation's earnings and a cost of capital.[3] Analysts typically derive the cost of capital by reference to long-term historical returns realized in the public

1 This guide will use the terms "pass-through entity" and "subchapter S corporation" interchangeably. However, we acknowledge that there are differences between S corporations and other forms of pass-through entities that might affect the magnitude of any value differential between it and the public market. See, for example, "Partnership-Audit Techniques Guide," www.irs.gov/Businesses/Partnerships/Partnership---Audit-Techniques-Guide-(ATG).

2 A market approach or a net asset approach may have entirely different considerations (such as, in the market approach, differences in multiples of transactions of S corporations versus C corporations; a net asset value approach may lead the analyst to the conclusion that the S corporation assets have built-in gains, such that a 338(h)(10) election may influence the value of the S corporation; for a complete discussion of the effect of a 338(h)(10) election on the S corporation, see Merle Erickson, "Tax Benefits in Acquisitions of Privately Held Corporations," *Capital Ideas*, Volume 3, No. 3, Winter 2002). However, these considerations are *different* than that which is presented in the models that the Tax Court, the IRS, and valuation analysts have employed and require a wholly alternative calculation.

3 The cost of capital typically obtained for use in the valuation of a pass-through entity is the same, regardless of the purposes of the valuation or the standard of value employed. This is important to note, as the Tax Court (and by extension, the IRS) has attempted to make a distinction between the effect of taxes on value in the context of a fair market value calculation and a fair value calculation. However, as analysts obtain their cost of capital from the same source irrespective of the standard of value, for purposes of our analysis, we view this as a distinction without a difference.

market. Thus, the reference throughout this discussion to a *public* C corporation, and not a private C corporation, is a critical distinction.[4]

In the application of the income approach, a return derived from publicly traded companies is used to value the closely held pass-through entity. However, there is a mismatch between the pass-through entity and the public-market return used to value it. Public companies pay taxes on corporate income, and, then, their investors pay personal taxes when they either receive income returns (dividends) or sell their stock. Comparatively, investors in pass-through entities pay personal-level taxes on passed-through corporate income but avoid further personal (dividend and capital gains) taxes. Therefore, this tax differential needs to be accounted for in the valuation of the pass-through entity.

A large portion of this guide is devoted to the findings of academic research related to the impact of taxes on value. This research demonstrates that the fact that public-market investors have to pay personal taxes on investment returns leads to a downward pressure on public-market stock prices (generally referred to in the literature as a "tax penalty"). If the public stock price is depressed because public shareholders have to pay personal taxes, then the return derived from it (as calculated by publicly available data providers such as Duff & Phelps) is too high to be applied to a company whose shareholders won't bear such personal taxes. This concept is illustrated in Exhibit 1-1, which assumes two publicly traded companies: one whose shareholders are not subject to dividend and capital gains taxes, and one whose shareholders are subject to these personal taxes.

Exhibit 1-1. Illustrative Example of the Impact on Value, and Capitalization Rate, of Personal Taxes in the Public Market

	No Personal Taxes	Impact of Personal Taxes on Value and Capitalization Rate
Stock value	$100,000	$80,000
Net income after corporate tax, but before shareholder tax	$12,000	$12,000
Price/Earnings ratio	8.3	6.7
Capitalization rate	12%	15%
Investor-level tax	0%	20%
Investor-level income	$12,000	$9,600
After-tax return on investment	12%	12%

4 Because the issue to be addressed is the impact of personal taxes on value in the public market versus the pass-through entity, any comparison to a private C corporation is irrelevant to this discussion (except to the extent that investors in private C corporations mimic a pass-through entity and similarly employ strategies to avoid or reduce personal taxes).

Using these figures (which are purely illustrative) as an example, the analyst (through the sources from which we obtain our cost of capital) would derive a capitalization rate of 15%, which would be appropriate to apply to a company whose shareholders incur personal (dividend and capital gains) taxes. However, this cost of capital would be too high to apply to a company whose shareholders do not incur taxes at the personal level, resulting in an undervaluation of a pass-through entity.

Because of this mismatch, valuation analysts have added a premium to the value of pass-through entities by employing various models designed by business valuation analysts (hereinafter referred to as the "S corp models"[5]).

Regardless of which of the S corp models the analyst employs, a simplified explanation of what the models accomplish is as follows: Using the example provided in Exhibit 1-1, and using a capitalization of income model, analysts would typically derive a value by dividing the net income of $12,000 (adjusted to reflect that investors in pass-through entities bear taxes on pass-through corporate income) by the public-market return of 15% and arrive at a value of $80,000. However, this value is thought to be too low, since the pass-through entity's investors will not bear personal (dividend and capital gains) taxes. Thus, analysts typically add a premium to their value determination to counter the effect of the tax penalty that is embedded in the public-market return.

Through the varying mechanisms employed by the S corp models, an analyst would typically arrive at a premium of up to 25%. This premium is then applied to the value determination of, in our example, $80,000, to arrive at a value conclusion of $100,000 ($80,000 times 1.25).

Exhibit 1-2 demonstrates the conceptual framework employed by the S corp models to determine the magnitude of the premium.

Exhibit 1-2. Conceptual Framework of S Corp Models

	Public C Corp	S Corp
Income before corporate tax	$100	$100
Corporate income tax rate	40%	0%
Available earnings	$60	$100
Taxes at personal level	20%	40%
Available after taxes at personal level	$48	$60
"Premium" per S corporation models		**25%**

The percentage difference between the cash available

5 A complete discussion of the various S corp models analysts have typically employed is not the subject of this guide and, as such, will not be addressed in detail. However, the S corp models all generally achieve the same, or similar, outcome and share a conceptual framework. That framework will be discussed at times throughout this guide. However, for an excellent summary and analysis of the most widely used models, see Shannon P. Pratt and David Laro, *Business Valuation and Federal Taxes: Procedure. Law and Perspective,* 2nd ed., John Wiley & Sons Inc., 2011.

to the public C corporation investor and the S corporation investor is then added to the pass-through entity value (that was derived by use of a public-market return).

Critical to this analysis is an understanding that the S corp models compare the income that is available to the public-market investor to that which is available to the pass-through entity investor. The method employed by the Delaware Chancery Court, discussed in Chapter 6, makes the same comparison. This comparison is relevant because we are attempting to resolve the mismatch between the return derived from the public market (typically a historical return dating back to 1926 or 1963, depending on the data used by the analyst) and the S corporation. However, analysts generally employ these models by assuming that the public-market return has embedded in it investor-level taxes at the rate of 20%. As this text will discuss, this assumption is not borne out by the research.

For example, assume that investors in the public C corp in Exhibit 1-2 were subject to an effective tax rate on their return of 10%, rather than 20%. In that case, the resulting required subchapter S premium is significantly smaller, as demonstrated in Exhibit 1-3.

Exhibit 1-3. Demonstration of Effect of Lower Dividend and Capital Gains Tax Rate

	Public C Corp	S Corp
Income before corporate tax	$100	$100
Corporate income tax rate	40%	0%
Available earnings	$60	$100
Taxes at personal level	10%	40%
Available after taxes at personal level	$54	$60
"Premium" per S corporation models		11%

The issue of how taxes affect the value of an S corporation gained significant recognition in 1999 with the Tax Court's decision in *Gross v. Commissioner*.[6] In that case, the Tax Court first examined and then rejected the concept of "tax affecting" (that is, allowing a deduction for taxes on corporate earnings) the earnings of a subchapter S corporation when using the income approach to estimate the fair market value of a firm (hereinafter referred to as "no tax affect model"). Absent the allowance of a deduction for taxes on corporate income, the indicated value resulting from the application of an income approach is as much as 67% greater than what it would be if taxes on corporate income were deducted. In short, explicitly following the Tax Court's decision will result in a very significant valuation differential between two otherwise identical companies if

6 *Gross v. Commissioner*, T.C. Memo 1999-254, aff'd, 272 F.3d 333 F.3d (6th Cir. 2001).

one is a public C corporation and the other is a pass-through entity.

There is a significant distinction between the theory underlying the Tax Court's holdings and the theory underlying the S corp models. The Tax Court has taken positions that would only be appropriate if personal taxes did not affect value (this is understandable, since they have never been presented with any evidence that they do). In contrast, the valuation profession has generally adopted a position whereby it acknowledges that personal taxes affect value. These disparate views are presented in

Exhibit 1-4.

Exhibit 1-4. No Tax Affect Model Compared to S Corp Models

	Public C Corp	S Corp	"Premium"
Income before corporate tax	$100.00	$100.00	
Corporate income tax rate	40%	0%	
Available earnings	$60.00	$100.00	
No tax affect model			**67%**
Taxes at personal level	20%	40%	
Available after taxes at personal level	$48.00	$60.00	
"Premium" per S corporation models			**25%**

The no tax affect model inherently assumes that shareholder taxes are irrelevant (whether they are dividend, capital gains, or income tax). The research discussed later in this guide will demonstrate that this assumption is false.

The distinction between the models is stark, with the no tax affect model resulting in a value determination that is in excess of 40% higher than that which one would derive using the S corp models. The academic literature discussed herein demonstrates that personal taxes do affect value, thereby supporting the position taken in the S corp models (and in contrast to the position generally taken in the no tax affect model). The failure to take these taxes into consideration generally results in an overstatement of value. However, the literature also reveals that the S corp models are also flawed, in that they overstate the magnitude of taxes actually incurred by public-market investors at the personal level, causing these models, too, to generally reach an overstated value conclusion.

The S corp models, which are widely used throughout the valuation profession, incorporate shareholder-level taxes *as if they were paid by public-market investors at the statutory rate*. However, the results of a stream of fruitful academic research clearly demonstrate that this most basic and critical assumption is flawed.

Investors in the public market seek to avoid or defer personal taxes, and many public-market investors pay no tax at all. The cost of capital derived from public-company returns represents a blend of returns that impound: (1) the types of income (dividend and capital gain) they provide their shareholders; (2) the mix of tax clienteles and marginal investors making up those shareholders; and (3) the tax regime in place at any given time for the mix of returns. The S corp models assume that the historical cost of capital is not this blending of investors but rather is made up of investors who are all taxed on dividend and capital gain income, who immediately pay dividend and capital gains tax at the statutory rates, and who take no actions to avoid paying these taxes. In reality, shareholder taxes are embedded in the cost of capital but at a rate that is less than the statutory rate. The failure to take this into account may, therefore, result in an overstated value conclusion when applied to a sub S corporation or other pass-through entity.

As Ayers et al. assert:

> The effect of shareholder-level taxes on stock prices is a fundamental issue for both tax policy and stock valuation. Shareholder-level taxes may affect share prices because these taxes are imposed on distributions of earnings (dividend taxes) and on the sale of shares through trades, share repurchases, and liquidating distributions (capital gains taxes), thus reducing the after-tax cash flows to investors.[7]

Given this, the critical question, and, indeed, the crux of this guide, is to address the question: To what extent have valuation analysts failed to correctly match cash flows with the appropriate cost of capital?

We next turn to a discussion of the concept of implicit taxes, which is the foundation upon which an understanding of the relationship of the cost of capital to pass-through entities is built.

7 Benjamin C. Ayers, Bryan C. Cloyd, and John R. Robinson, "The Effect of Shareholder-Level Dividend Taxes on Stock Prices: Evidence From the Revenue Reconciliation Act of 1993," *The Accounting Review*, October 2002, Vol. 77, No. 4.

Chapter 2. Introduction to the Concept of Implicit Taxes

Chapters 4 and 5 contain an extensive discussion of research on the impact of taxes on asset values and returns. To fully appreciate and evaluate the implications of that line of research, it is helpful to gain familiarity with several important and persuasive concepts embodied in these studies.

When one discusses income taxes, one typically thinks about taxes paid to a taxing authority. Such taxes are commonly referred to as "explicit taxes," and readers are generally comfortable with their understanding of these taxes. However, the concept of "implicit taxes" may be less familiar to many readers. A comparison of taxable versus tax-exempt bonds is helpful in understanding these concepts. While a comparison of the tax attributes of bonds is more simplified than a comparison of the tax attributes of a public C corporation to an S corporation, the lessons gained from the bond market demonstrate the framework for the concepts discussed in this guide (and, in fact, it is upon bond pricing theory that the S corp models were built).

Taxable versus tax-exempt bonds. Implicit taxes can be measured as the difference in pre-shareholder tax return that a fully taxable investment and an identical, tax-favored investment generate. The classic example would be the difference in rates of return on a fully taxable bond and an otherwise identical tax-exempt municipal bond. Financial analysts are familiar with the fact that the market prices taxable bonds to yield higher returns than similar tax-exempt bonds. In short, investors buying the tax-exempt bonds are willing to make the trade-off between: (1) lower returns; and (2) tax-exempt income. However, in reality, the analysis is a bit more involved.

We generally calculate the value of a bond as a function of:

1. The amount and timing of future payments of interest and principal; and
2. The market discount rate, or required rate of return on a bond with that risk profile.

When evaluating differences in values between bonds with identical coupon rates, maturity, etc., financial texts will emphasize that the most critical factor in differences in the market discount rate is risk. The market should price bonds with identical payment features and identical risk by using identical discount rates, yielding identical values. However, this conclusion clearly would not hold when comparing identical taxable and tax-exempt bonds as the tax-exempt bonds will be priced higher, implying a lower required rate of return. However, the readily observable rate of return on bonds, as reflected by their price, measures only pretax return to the investor. The key to evaluating the impact of the taxes on the bonds is to evaluate *after-tax returns*, as we do with the following example.

Assume that a taxable bond sells for a price yielding a 10% return. If the tax rate on bond income (t) is 30%, an investor in the bond will derive the after-tax return according to Exhibit 2-1.

Exhibit 2-1. Taxable Bond

	Taxable Bond
Pretax return on taxable bond	10%
Investor-level taxes on bond income (explicit taxes)	30%
After-tax return [Pretax return x (1-t)]	7%

Note that there are two return metrics here, a pretax return and an after-tax return, with tax in this case referring solely to investor-level taxes.[8] Both are accurate measures, but due to explicit taxes it is important to differentiate these alternative return measures. By extension, when referring to either return measure, it is critical to always specify which is being described.

By expanding this simple analysis to include an identical tax-exempt bond, we can examine the impact of implicit taxes on security prices. If we assume that investor-level taxes have no impact on bond prices (similar to the assumption the no tax affect model has made with respect to public C corporation [taxable] versus S corporation [nontaxable]), we would expect to see the pricing for identical taxable and tax-exempt bonds as shown in Exhibit 2-2.

8 There has been some confusion in valuation literature about the meaning of the term "pretax" when referencing returns. Public-market returns are generally expressed as *preinvestor-level taxes* (and are thus "pretax"), but post taxes paid at the corporate level.

Exhibit 2-2. Taxable Versus Tax-Exempt Bond (Assuming Taxes Do Not Impact Pricing)		
	Taxable Bond	Tax Exempt Bond
Pretax return on taxable bond	10%	10%
Investor-level taxes on bond income (explicit taxes)	30%	0%
After-tax return [pretax return x (1-t)]	7%	10%

If investors focus only on pretax returns, they would be indifferent between the alternative investments and would price them identically. By extension, tax-exempt bonds would trade at similar prices and yields as taxable bonds. However, if investors are sensitive to investor-level taxes, we would logically expect the pricing relationships shown in Exhibit 2-3.

Exhibit 2-3. Taxable Versus Tax-Exempt Bond (Reflecting Impact of Taxes on Pricing)		
	Taxable Bond	Tax Exempt Bond
Pretax return on taxable bond	10%	7%
Investor-level taxes on bond income (explicit taxes)	30%	0%
After-tax return [pretax return x (1-t)]	7%	7%

If investors seek to reduce explicit taxes on their investment income, they will naturally bid the price of the tax-exempt bond up, reducing pretax returns on the tax-exempt bond relative to the taxable bond. This process should logically continue until the after-tax yield on the tax-exempt bond equals that of the fully taxable bond, and this is what we observe in the bond market. This concept is demonstrated in Exhibit 2-4.

Exhibit 2-4. Pricing of Taxable Versus Tax-Exempt Bond		
	Taxable Bond	Tax Exempt Bond
Price	$1,000	$1,425
Pretax return on taxable bond	10.0%	7.0%
Pretax cash flow	$100	$100
Investor level tax	30.0%	0.0%
Investor level income	$70	$100
After-tax return on investment	7.0%	7.0%

While the tax-exempt bond still bears no explicit taxes, investors face a different tax, known as an implicit tax. All other things being equal, due to the implicit tax created by the market seeking to maximize after-tax returns, fully taxable investors face a choice between a 30% explicit tax and a 30% implicit tax, and such investors will be indifferent as to which bond they purchase.

Any competent tax advisor will tell certain clients to consider tax-exempt bonds while advising other clients to avoid them completely. The important consideration is *the relative tax situation of the client-investors*. We refer to clients in any given tax situation as "tax clienteles." For purposes of our discussion, let's assume we have two tax clienteles:

1. Investors with a 30% marginal tax rate; and
2. Investors with a 0% marginal tax rate.

Given this scenario, which investors will buy which bonds? To answer the question, one must evaluate after-tax returns.

If an investor with a 30% marginal rate buys either bond, a 7% after-tax return on investment will be received. In that case, the investor would be indifferent as to which bond to purchase. However, the investor with a 0% marginal rate would have a clear preference for the fully taxable bond. Due to the investor's tax situation, a 10% after-tax return will be earned, but only by investing in the fully taxable bond. By buying the tax-exempt bond, the investor pays the implicit tax, reducing the after-tax return (as we will discuss later in this guide, the same phenomenon can be seen in nontaxed investors, such as pension funds' preference for high-yield stocks).

In this example, the clientele with a 30% marginal rate is indifferent between the two investments. However, what if Congress were to lower the investors' tax rate to 20%? Would they now buy only fully taxable bonds since this would provide them with an 8% after-tax return versus the tax-exempt bond return of 7%?

Exhibit 2-5. Taxable (20%) Versus Tax-Exempt Bond

	Taxable Bond	Tax Exempt Bond
Pretax return on taxable bond	10%	7%
Investor-level taxes on bond income (explicit taxes)	20%	0%
After-tax return [pretax return x (1-t)]	8%	7%

Clienteles with high marginal rates would certainly be more attracted to the taxable bonds now, but market forces would ensure that equilibrium would once again be established. The investors with high marginal rates who were previously indifferent to the two alternative investments now seek the taxable bond with its high after-tax return. This clientele would bid the price for the taxable bonds up, eventually reducing its after-tax yield back to the market-determined rate of 7%.

The effect on the net after-tax yield, assuming a face value of $1,000 for both the taxable and the tax-exempt bond, is presented in Exhibit 2-7.

Exhibit 2-6. Taxable Versus Tax-Exempt Bond Returns - 20% Investor Tax Rate		
	Taxable Bond	Tax Exempt Bond
Pretax return on taxable bond	8.75%	7%
Investor-level taxes on bond income (explicit taxes)	20%	0%
After-tax return [pretax return x (1-t)]	7%	7%

Exhibit 2-7. Pricing of Yield on Taxable Versus Tax-Exempt Bond		
	Taxable Bond	Tax Exempt Bond
Price	$1,000	$1,000
Pretax return on taxable bond	8.8%	7.0%
Pretax cash flow	$88	$70
Investor level tax	20.0%	0.0%
Investor level income	$70	$70
After-tax return on investment	7.0%	7.0%

At this point, the driving force behind the setting of taxable bond prices is the tax rate on the investors with high marginal rates. Since they are setting the price, we can refer to them as the *marginal investor*, or price setter, for that investment during that period. Note that this process would directly impact the pricing of the bonds. This is demonstrated in Exhibit 2-8.

Exhibit 2-8. Pricing of Taxable Versus Tax-Exempt Bonds		
	Taxable Bond	Tax Exempt Bond
Price	$800	$1,000
Pretax return on taxable bond	8.75%	7.0%
Pretax cash flow	$70	$70
Investor level tax	20.0%	0.0%
Investor level income	$56	$70
After-tax return on investment	7.0%	7.0%

The tax-exempt bond will require a lower pretax yield than the taxable bond in order to produce the same pretax cash flows as the taxable bond; as a result, the tax-exempt bond will be priced higher.

Not surprisingly, and as is discussed in Chapters 4 and 5, this same pricing phenomenon can be seen in the public stock markets from which analysts obtain their cost of capital. Data clearly demonstrate that shareholder taxes on the income of publicly traded equities impact the prices of those equities. Thus, any measure of cost of capital derived from publicly traded company data must be evaluated in light of shareholder-level taxes.

Lessons from the bond markets. From this set of simple examples we can draw the following conclusions:

1. Investors will minimize explicit taxes by investing in tax-favored investments but only to the extent that explicit tax savings do not exceed marginal implicit taxes.
2. The market will pursue an equilibrium after-tax rate of return. Thus, returns that are after shareholder taxes, rather than pretax returns, determine the pricing of investments.
3. Investments that are tax favored in any way will bear implicit taxes in the form of reduced pretax returns. Investors purchasing these investments will "pay" the implicit tax regardless of their explicit tax situation (tax clientele).
4. Various tax clienteles exist and will naturally be drawn to investments with tax attributes that best benefit a given clientele (maximize after-tax return).
5. At any point in time, there may be a marginal investor for a given investment as a clientele attempts to exploit a lack of equilibrium. The marginal investor for a given investment may change with changes in tax rates on various investments, changes in tax rates on various clienteles, changes in the mix of returns derived from a given investment, or changes in the market rates of return.

Perhaps the most critical of these observations is that after-tax cash flows to the investor drive market prices (and therefore the returns we derive therefrom). This is critical in that all widely accepted models used to estimate required rates of return on equity inherently incorporate the effects on pricing of investor-level taxes. When we observe historical dividends and changes in market prices and use these to calculate historical returns, we have heretofore presumed that these returns have been measured before shareholder-level taxes. However, this presumption is not accurate. Changes in investor-level taxes can directly impact investment prices and, therefore, returns.

This is a sobering thought for analysts attempting to discern the magnitude that such shareholder taxes have on the calculated historical return, given the innumerable changes made in our tax code over the past century. These returns impound the effects of numerous changes in shareholder-level taxes. Additionally, the market prices and returns that we observe over time have been set by an array of constantly changing tax clienteles and, by extension, marginal investors.

Do these rather simple analyses and resulting conclusions appear to hold under actual market conditions? As we will describe throughout this guide, the answer is "yes." One of the clearest examples of this was a study that examined the impact on stock prices when Canada rather unexpectedly announced changes in the taxation of Canadian income trusts. The new tax law eliminated certain tax preferences on income from these trusts. This would be similar to our analysis if we were to assume that the tax-exempt bond would immediately become fully taxable. Our analysis would conclude that investors would no longer be satisfied with the relatively low pretax return and would bid the price down as a means of increasing both pre- and posttax returns. In fact, using the examples provided earlier in this chapter, to achieve equilibrium, the pretax yield would have to increase to 10% (resulting in a decrease in the price). In their analysis of Canada's tax law change, Edwards and Shevlin found that prices decreased by 13% during the three-day period surrounding the announcement.[9] Note that the tax law did not impact pretax returns to investors, only their after-tax returns. This (along with other studies discussed later in this guide) provides very strong evidence that investor-level taxes have a profound effect on investment values and returns.

Summary. The theory is fairly straightforward. Theoretically, one should be able to adjust observed market returns to measure a more "pure" return, either pretax or after tax. We can generally do this for bonds. However, equities present more challenges, including:

- The mix of returns (dividend and capital gain) with different tax attributes;
- The mix of returns changing over time;
- The mix of tax regimes over time;
- The mix of market participants and tax clienteles over time;
- The fact that it is difficult to observe implicit taxes on equities;
- That it is difficult to measure explicit taxes on capital gains, since they can be deferred indefinitely by certain clienteles;
- That it is difficult to identify tax clienteles; and
- That it is difficult to identify marginal investors.

Despite these difficulties and challenges, academic research has undertaken substantial efforts to examine these effects, providing analysts with some tools to better estimate a required rate of return on equity than our current mixed measure.

We now turn to the implications of taxes on the cost of capital.

9 Alexander Edwards and Terry Shevlin, "The Value of a Flow-Through Entity in an Integrated Corporate Tax System," *Journal of Financial Economics*, 2011, Vol. 101, Issue 2, pp. 473-491.

Chapter 3. An Explanation of the Implications of Shareholder Taxes on the Corporate Cost of Capital

Estimates of the cost of equity are distressingly imprecise.

—*Eugene F. Fama and Kenneth R. French*[10]

Recalling the various assumptions underlying the two positions presented in Exhibit 1-4, the no tax affect model assumes that taxes on corporate-level income borne at the shareholder level do not affect value at all. However, research clearly demonstrates that shareholder-level taxes do affect value. This chapter will provide an explanation of how.

In 1977, Merton Miller, a Nobel Prize winner in economics, introduced the effects of personal taxes on investment returns and capital structure in his seminal work, "Debt and Taxes."[11] Miller argued that investors base their returns on the after-personal-tax returns of various investments. Consider the basic equity valuation model in Equation 1.

Equation 1. Equity Valuation Model

$$Ve = \sum_{t=0}^{\infty} \frac{CFe_t}{(1+r)^t} \cdots > 0$$

where:

Ve = the value of equity;

CFe_t = the expected net (after-tax) cash flows to equity during period t; and

r = the investor/shareholder's required after-tax rate of return.

10 Eugene F. Fama and Kenneth R. French, "Industry Costs of Equity," *Journal of Financial Economics*, Vol. 43 Issue 2 (1997), pp. 153-193.

11 Merton H. Miller, "Debt and Taxes," *Journal of Finance*, May 1977, Volume 32, No. 2, pages 267-270.

Corporate income taxes clearly affect firm value to the extent that they impact the timing of projected net cash flows (t), the amount of projected net cash flows (CF), the discount rate/required rate of return (r), or any combination of these factors. Thus, changes in corporate tax rates should have an impact on the value of corporate equity to the extent they impact cash flows, rates of return, or both.

While not explicitly shown in Equation 1, shareholder-level taxes also impact corporate investment decisions, though not directly, but rather through their impact on the corporate cost of equity capital. The impact of shareholder-level taxes on corporate equity returns can be demonstrated by comparing the corporate cost of capital in a tax-free environment to that of a traditional double-tax environment. For purposes of simplicity, we consider a pure-equity (unlevered) firm.[12] In the absence of shareholder-level taxes, the equilibrium corporate cost of equity capital should be equal to the combined expected rate of return to shareholders from dividends and share price appreciation.[13] This tax-free equilibrium is depicted in Equation 2.

Equation 2. Tax-Free Equilibrium Model

$$Ce = Rs = Rd + Rcg$$

where:

Ce = corporate cost of equity;
Rs = expected total after-tax returns to shareholders;
Rd = expected shareholder pretax returns in the form of dividends; and
Rcg = expected shareholder pretax returns in the form of share appreciation (capital gain).

Rs, the market return to shareholders, is set by the market. Thus, when shareholder-level taxes are imposed, shareholder pretax returns must increase in order for shareholder total after-tax returns (Rs) to remain constant. Unlike their relation in the tax-free environment, the corporate cost of equity and total shareholder after-tax returns now differ by the amount of total explicit shareholder-level taxes. The relationship between individual shareholder taxes and the corporate cost of equity capital under a traditional double-taxation system, in equilibrium, is represented in Equation 3.

12 Due to the difference in taxation of dividends and interest, corporate tax policy also impacts corporate financing decisions. See Craig T. Schulman, Deborah W. Thomas, Keith F. Sellers, and Duane B. Kennedy, "Effects of Tax Integration and Capital Gains Tax on Corporate Leverage," *National Tax Journal*, 1996, 49 (1): 31-54, for an examination of the effects of dividend imputation on equilibrium debt-to-equity ratios and the cost of debt financing.

13 Consistent with Morningstar (*Yale ICF Working Paper No. 00-44*, 2002), which provides an excellent discussion and empirical examination of the corporate cost of capital and its linkage to expected shareholder returns, we use required "rate of return" and "cost of capital" synonymously.

Equation 3. Shareholder-Level Tax Equilibrium Model

$$Ce - Ts = Rs = Rd(1 - Td) + Rcg(1 - Tcg)$$

where:

Ts = total shareholder-level tax rate;

Td = shareholder tax rate on dividend income; and

Tcg = shareholder tax rate on capital gains, and all other terms are as defined above.

Equation 3 suggests that if the effective tax rates on dividends and/or capital gains increase, the pretax return required to earn a constant after-tax return also increases. Under such a system, the corporation's cost of equity capital differs from the shareholders' after-tax return by the amount of expected shareholder-level taxes on dividends, Rd × Td, plus the amount of expected shareholder-level taxes on capital gains, Rcg × Tcg.

To demonstrate the impact of shareholder-level taxes on corporate cost of equity, we can calculate cost of equity using Equation 3 as shown in Exhibit 3-1 below. Assume that Rs, the after-tax return to shareholders, has been set by the market at 10%. Also assume that a company currently provides half of that return in the form of dividends (Rd) and half in the form of capital gains (Rcg). In the absence of any shareholder taxes on either dividends or capital gains (column 1), the pretax and post-tax return to shareholders is 10% and the corporation's cost of equity is 10%.

Exhibit 3-1. Calculation of Cost of Equity: Impact of Shareholder-Level Taxes

	No Taxes	Tax on Dividends and Capital Gains	Dissimilar Tax Rates on Dividends and Capital Gains	Return Mix Adjusted to Reduce Cost of Capital
Market set after-tax return (constant)	10.00%	10.00%	10.00%	10.00%
Returns Before-Shareholder Taxes				
Returns from dividends (Rd)	5.00%	6.25%	6.25%	2.50%
Returns from capital gains (Rcg)	5.00%	6.25%	5.56%	8.89%
Total pretax return to shareholders	10.00%	12.50%	11.81%	11.39%
Shareholder Tax Rates				
Dividend tax rates (Td)	0.00%	20.00%	20.00%	20.00%
Capital gains tax rates (Tcg)	0.00%	20.00%	10.00%	10.00%
Returns After-Shareholder Taxes				
After-tax dividend return	5.00%	5.00%	5.00%	2.00%
After-tax capital gain return	5.00%	5.00%	5.00%	8.00%
Total after-tax return to shareholders	10.00%	10.00%	10.00%	10.00%
Cost of equity capital	10.00%	12.50%	11.81%	11.39%

However, if a tax rate of 20% is now imposed on both dividends (Td) and capital gains (Tcg), the pretax return must increase in order to maintain the 10% after-tax return to shareholders. As shown in column 2, the increase in pretax return will simultaneously increase the cost of equity capital for the corporation to 12.50%.

But what if the tax rates on dividends and capital gains are different, as in column 3? The lower tax rate on capital gains reduces the cost of capital somewhat. More importantly, this difference provides an opportunity (and incentive) for the company to change its dividend policy. If it reduces dividends and increases the return via capital gains, the overall pretax return, and cost of equity, can be reduced while maintaining the total market set return to investors. In this case, by reducing pretax dividend returns to 2.5% and increasing pretax capital gain returns to 8.89% (through share buybacks, for example), the shareholders will receive their sought-after 10% return, while the corporation's cost of equity capital is reduced from 11.81% to 11.39%. This model helps explain what research has clearly demonstrated: Over the past 50 years, public corporations in the U.S. have used massive share buybacks rather than dividends to put cash into the hands of their shareholders while lowering their cost of capital.

It is important to note that Td and Tcg are neither observable nor constant across shareholders or over time. Not only are tax rates on dividend income progressive for individuals (at least historically), but also a very large percentage of stocks are held by tax-deferred and tax-exempt vehicles such as traditional and Roth IRAs. The same is true for the effective capital gains tax rates, the calculation of which is even more difficult due to the availability of unlimited deferral. Various tax clienteles will naturally concentrate their investments in appropriate stocks based on their tax positions, as well as the expected amounts and form of returns.

This clientele effect, combined with variations in the timing of dividend distributions and shareholder control over the timing of capital gains, make marginal rates for these taxes, measures of expected shareholder after-tax returns, and cost of equity capital difficult to calculate with precision. This said, Scholes et al. estimated relative required rates of return for corporations and partnerships during the years surrounding the Jobs and Growth Tax Relief Reconciliation Act of 2003 (JGTRRA) and concluded that cost of corporate capital should have dropped. By comparing rates of return on dividends and capital gains while assuming a 10% pretax return on partnership income, they conclude that:

> Lowering the tax on dividends from 35% to 15% for a firm paying out 100% of earnings (in the form of dividends) reduces the firm's cost of capital from 15.38% to 11.76%. Lowering the capital gains rate for a non-dividend-paying firm also lowers its cost of capital. Further, the cost of capital is still lower for non-dividend-paying firms even

when *Td* = *Tcg* because of the effects of tax deferral on capital gains.[14]

The preceding discussion highlights two critical points. First, there is strong analytical support for assertions that taxes on dividends and capital gains impact the corporate cost of equity capital. Second, Scholes et al. highlight the difficulty in quantifying the actual expected impact, due to the confounding effects of variations in: (1) expected dividend-payout policies; (2) expected holding periods; and (3) shareholder tax clienteles.

We now turn to the research that establishes, first, that shareholder taxes affect value and, second, that numerous factors work to mute the extent to which taxes in the public markets affect value.

14 Myron S. Scholes, Mark Wolfson, Merle Erickson, Edward Maydew, and Terrence Shevlin, *Taxes and Business Strategy: A Planning Approach*, 2009, Englewood Cliffs, N.J.: Prentice-Hall, p. 108.

Chapter 4. Literature Review: Research on the Effect of Taxes Embedded in the Cost of Capital

> It is important to understand the degree to which investor taxes are impounded into security prices, which in turn can affect investment returns, the cost of capital, capital structure, and investment spending.
>
> —*Franklin Allen and Roni Michaely*[15]

Empirical Research in Accounting and Capital Markets

As readers will soon appreciate, this guide differs significantly from many professional publications in that its foundations rest squarely on a wealth of empirical academic research on the relationships between taxes, cost of capital, and share prices. As an academic who has both studied and published research studies on these topics, and, as a practitioner who has researched these topics extensively, we are well acquainted with significant contributions such research can provide the valuation profession, as well as its limitations.

First and foremost, readers should be aware of the incredible amount of thought and effort that goes into the type of research relied upon in this guide. Before a research paper can even be considered for publication in a premier journal, the authors must thoroughly develop the underlying theory, carefully collect and evaluate data, devise numerous statistical analyses and tests, and evaluate the results of their research. It is not unusual for this process to take many months of work. However, that is only the beginning.

Even a very well-designed study utilizing very advanced analytical analyses faces huge obstacles before it can be published. All premier journals require a double-blind review process, with the reviewers selected from outstanding scholars in the area. The review process is far more than a simple accept/reject decision. Rather, it is a process that helps researchers improve, refine, and hopefully perfect their study. Statistics from the editor of *The Accounting Review*, widely considered to be one of the top five academic accounting journals, give an idea of the excellence required of a study before it is published.

15 Franklin Allen and Roni Michaely, "Payout Policy," *Guide of the Economics of Finance*, Edited by G.M. Constantinides, M. Harris, and R. Stulz (Elsevier B.V. 2003), p. 339.

Outcome of 501 Articles Submitted During 12 Months Ending May 31, 2011		
Total research papers submitted	501	100.0%
Rejected outright	380	75.8%
Uncertain—fate to be determined by editor and reviewers	54	10.8%
Invited to revise the manuscript and resubmit	64	12.8%
Accept or conditional accept for publication	3	0.6%

As can be seen, the odds of simply submitting an article and having it accepted for publication are well under 1%. While the majority of the papers are rejected outright, about 25% are in limbo after they have been reviewed. If the preliminary decision is "uncertain," it generally means that at least one reviewer believes the paper has potential but another feels that the research is "flawed." These papers will most likely be rejected. If the authors are invited to "revise and resubmit," it means that the reviewers believe the research has the potential to make a significant contribution to our knowledge but needs significant additional work (for example, need additional data or measured differently, new statistical tests, etc.). In any event, of the 500 to 600 articles submitted each year, approximately 15% are eventually published.

In summary, readers should appreciate the rigor that is found in this type of research. On the other hand, readers should also know that most research represents an attempt to study a very narrow question, fact, or relationship. As every valuation analyst knows, real world data are messy. Researchers try to limit the "noise" found in data by focusing on narrow issues. This does not invalidate the research, but it explains why so many studies have examined various aspects of the tax cost of capital issue, while few, if any, have attempted to look at a unified model of the relationships. Our goal with this guide has been to cull through the voluminous research on the effects of taxes on value and present practical applications of it that analysts can use in making their value determinations.

Empirical evidence linking shareholder-level taxes to business value. A wealth of published research examines the relationship between taxes, security prices, and the cost of equity capital. While a full discussion of this research is beyond the scope of this guide, certain key studies provide important evidence and are discussed in depth. Researchers originally endeavored to determine the extent to which both dividend and capital gains taxes affect value. Over time, as the complexity of these relationships became apparent, research has focused on what factors impact the relationship between taxes, firm value, and cost of capital. We begin our discussion with a review of the literature relating to the capitalization of dividend taxes into share price.

Dividend tax capitalization. In the context of dividend and capital gains taxes and their impact on public share prices, tax capitalization is generally defined as "the effect of taxes on prices when current prices are lower than they otherwise would be because of future explicit taxes on those assets."[16] Existing studies use a variety of methods to test both the existence and magnitude of dividend tax capitalization.

16 Edward L. Maydew, "Empirical Tax Research in Accounting: A Discussion," *Journal of Accounting and Economics*, September 2001, Vol. 31, Nos. 1-3, p. 9.

Ex-dividend date studies test whether stock price adjustments on ex-dividend days reflect taxes on dividends.[17] In particular, one study found that, "on average, the price of a share of common stock on the ex-dividend day falls by less than the amount of the dividend (resulting in a positive stock return), and this result has been attributed to the fact that dividends are taxed at a higher rate than capital gains."[18] In other words, not only do shareholder taxes impact share value, the relative tax rates on various forms of return are important.

Early studies on the effect of dividend taxes on stock prices had mixed and controversial results, especially as later studies built on their findings.[19] Stocks that yield the lowest dividends attract investors in the higher tax brackets, and high dividend-yield stocks attract investors in lower tax brackets, which mitigate the tax effect of dividends in the equity rate.[20] Authors of one study add that marginal investors may be tax-exempt.[21] Studies further suggest that investors could escape the dividend tax penalty altogether by levering their purchases of equities, offsetting taxable dividends with interest deductions.[22]

Two studies concluded that the present value of shareholder-dividend tax is capitalized in price.[23] However, a subsequent study questioned these findings in light of: (1) tax clienteles (that is, the ownership of dividend-paying firms by a combination of taxable, tax-favored, and nontaxable entities); and (2) empirical observations that many firms rarely pay dividends at all.[24] Although these studies have been built on and expanded in later years, they laid the foundation for the myriad of issues that affect dividend tax capitalization—including the effects of varying payout strategies, clienteles, and different tax rates across different years and investors.

17 David A. Guenther, "Investor Reaction to Anticipated 1997 Capital Gains Tax Rate Reduction," working paper, 1999, Boulder, Colo.: University of Colorado, referring to E. Elton and M. Gruber, "Marginal Stockholder Tax Rates and the Clientele Effect," *Review of Economics and Statistics*, 1970, 52: 68-74; A. Kalay, "The Ex-Dividend Day Behavior of Stock Prices: A Re-Examination of the Clientele Effect," *Journal of Finance*, 1982, Vol. 37, pp. 1059-1070.

18 David A. Guenther, "Investor Reaction to Anticipated 1997 Capital Gains Tax Rate Reduction," working paper, 1999, Boulder, Colo.: University of Colorado, p. 1.

19 As discussed below, much of this can be explained by changes in tax regimes and tax clienteles over time.

20 Dan Dhaliwal, Linda Krull, Oliver Zhen Li, and William Moser, "Dividend Taxes and the Implied Cost of Equity Capital," *Journal of Accounting Research*, December 2005, Vol. 43, No. 5, p. 680.

21 Ibid., Elsevier, citing M. Miller and M. Scholes, "Dividend and Taxes: Some Empirical Evidence," *Journal of Political Economy*, 1982, Vol. 90, pp. 1118-41.

22 Miller and Scholes (1979); Robert H. Litzenberger and Krishna Ramaswamy, "Dividends, Short Selling Restrictions, Tax-Induced Investor Clienteles and Market Equilibrium," *The Journal of Finance*, May 1980, Vol. 35, No. 2, p. 470.

23 James Poterba and Lawrence Summers, "The Economic Effects of Dividend Taxation," NBER Working Paper No. 1353 (Also Reprint No. r0613), June 1985; George Zodrow, "On the 'Traditional' and 'New' Views of Dividend Taxation," *National Tax Journal*, 1991, p. 64.

24 Michelle Hanlon, James Myers, and Terry Shevlin, "Dividend Taxes and Firm Valuation: A Re-Examination," working paper, *SSRN*, June 4, 2001.

Some studies have focused on common stock returns surrounding major tax law changes affecting shareholder-level taxes such as changes in tax rates on dividends and capital gains.[25] These tax changes provide an ideal opportunity to directly observe the effect of shareholder-level taxes on firm prices, as well as firm and investor behavior. Studying the effects of the Revenue Reconciliation Act of 1993, Ayers et al. find that "the higher the firm's dividend yield, the more negative the firm's stock price reaction to the increase in the individual income tax rate (i.e., the dividend tax rate)"; they further find that the presence of institutional investors mitigate this negative reaction.[26]

All else being equal, if dividend taxes are lowered, share price should increase and the cost of capital should be lowered.[27] Several studies reported that, following the 2003 tax reforms that dropped the rate on dividend taxation, this was the case.[28] Another study found that the decrease in the dividend rate failed to boost stock values overall, but it did boost the values of high dividend-paying stocks, though not for a sustained time.[29] This is likely because, when tax rates change, investors (including possibly a newly created tax clientele) shift strategies so as to maximize their return.

Equity investments are priced in the public markets based on expected returns. When we calculate historical returns, we are in reality measuring expected return plus or minus unexpected return, resulting in a very noisy measure of expected return. In their 2005 study, Dhaliwal et al. challenged all of the previous studies—which relied on historical (ex post) returns to support theories of tax capitalization—by testing for dividend tax capitalization using an expected (ex ante) required return.[30] This is an important distinction for private-company valuation because the extent of the capitalization of the tax effect varies depending on the market return the analyst selects.[31,32] Using data

25 See Benjamin C. Ayers, Bryan C. Cloyd, and John R. Robinson, "The Effect of Shareholder-Level Dividend Taxes on Stock Prices: Evidence From the Revenue Reconciliation Act of 1993," *The Accounting Review*, October 2002, Vol. 77, No. 4; Mark Lang and Douglas Shackelford, "Capitalization of Capital Gains Taxes: Evidence From Stock Price Reactions to the 1997 Rate Reduction," *Journal of Public Economics*, April 2000, Vol.76, Issue 1, p.69-85.

26 Benjamin C. Ayers, Bryan C. Cloyd, and John R. Robinson, "The Effect of Shareholder-Level Dividend Taxes on Stock Prices: Evidence From the Revenue Reconciliation Act of 1993, *The Accounting Review*, October 2002, Vol. 77 No. 4, p. 933.

27 Randall Morck and Bernard Yeung, "Dividend Taxation and Corporate Governance," *Journal of Economic Perspectives*, Summer 2005, Volume 19, Number 3, p. 167.

28 Ibid., citing Blouin, Raedy, and Shackelford, 2004; Brown, Liang, and Weisbenner, 2004; and Chetty and Saez, 2004.

29 Gene Amromin, Paul Harrison, and Steven Sharpe, "How Did the 2003 Dividend Tax Cut Affect Stock Prices?" Finance and Economics Discussion Paper No. 2005-61, 2005.

30 Dan Dhaliwal, Linda Krull, Oliver Zhen Li, and William Moser, "Dividend Taxes and the Implied Cost of Equity Capital," *Journal of Accounting Research*, December 2005, Vol. 43, No. 5, p. 696.

31 Dan Dhaliwal, Linda Krull, Oliver Zhen Li, and William Moser, "Dividend Taxes and the Implied Cost of Equity Capital," *Journal of Accounting Research*, December 2005, Vol. 43, No. 5, p. 696.

32 Private-market valuation analysts typically rely on a market returns based on historical stock data. However, there are many ways to develop a return, including forward-looking methods, historical methods based on

from *Compustat*, the Center for Research in Security Prices, I/B/E/S, and Thompson Financial 13f Institutional Holdings, the authors found that the relation between cost of equity capital and dividend yield increases along with the dividend tax penalty. In other words, as the presence of dividend taxes increase, equity prices are penalized (e.g., they are lower), causing the cost of capital derived from such equity pricing to be higher than it would be without the presence of such taxes. In an additional important finding, their results also suggest that institutional investors serve to reduce this positive relationship.[33]

Furthermore, Dhaliwal et al. found that a higher tax rate on dividends relative to capital gains taxes increases the cost of equity capital, and this positive relation is a function of the tax attributes of the marginal investor.[34] This finding, which several other studies support, is critical in that it shows that not only are dividend taxes important, but dividend taxes of the *marginal investor for a given security* are also important. Thus, use of the statutory tax rate as a proxy for dividend tax rates will result in an erroneous measure to the extent that some taxpayers pay less than the statutory tax rate on dividends.

The authors conclude that the dividend tax effect is an important component of a firm's cost of equity capital[35] and that investor expectations regarding potential changes in tax rates introduce noise into the empirical analysis. Specifically, "if investors are uncertain about future tax rates, they may place less weight on the tax effect of dividends."[36] Finally, these authors found that the coefficient on dividend yield was highest when the tax penalty was highest (pre-Economic Recovery Tax Act) and that the coefficient on dividend yield changed consistently with tax law changes. These later studies continue to find that the dividend tax is capitalized into share price in the public market and that the magnitude of the effect on price (value) is influenced by many factors, but particularly:

- Clienteles (in particular, institutional investors);
- Company-specific payout policies; and
- Tax rates among investors.

alternate time horizons, survey methods, and others. The amount of tax effects that are "baked into" any particular derivation of a return will vary, depending on the data and assumptions used to develop it.

33 Dan Dhaliwal, Linda Krull, Oliver Zhen Li, and William Moser, "Dividend Taxes and the Implied Cost of Equity Capital," *Journal of Accounting Research*, December 2005, Vol. 43, No. 5, p. 696. This finding is critical in that it explains much of the variability in results from earlier studies. In essence, failure to control for clientele effects across firms and over time can lead to erroneous conclusions.

34 Dan Dhaliwal, Linda Krull, Oliver Zhen Li, and William Moser, "Dividend Taxes and the Implied Cost of Equity Capital," *Journal of Accounting Research*, December 2005, Vol. 43, No. 5, p. 697.

35 Ibid., p. 698.

36 Ibid.

This line of research demonstrates that dividend taxes are impounded into share price (and, therefore, the cost of capital we derive therefrom). Further, the research demonstrates that the extent to which share price is impacted is muted by the growing presence of institutional investors, as well as strategies firms and investors employ to reduce the impact of taxes.

So far the review of prior research has focused on studies of the relationship between dividend policy, dividend taxes, and firm value. In the next section, we examine the academic research focusing on the impact of capital gains taxes and firm value.

Capitalization of capital gains tax in equity price. Liang et al. found that stock prices reflect investor-level capital gains taxes. Specifically, stock prices react to changes in capital gains rates.[37] This finding is supported by a Congressional Budget Office study that found that "statistical results confirm earlier research findings that higher marginal tax rates on capital gains lower realizations of capital gains. The results are consistent with the widely held view that any overall revenue pickup from raising capital gains taxes is considerably less than the static pickup."[38] That is, tax revenue increases are not proportional to the increases in capital gain tax rates because the increase in the capital gains tax rate causes stock prices to drop and the holding period to increase (thereby decreasing gains subject to taxation).

Liang et al. further found that stocks with a longer holding period and dividend-paying stocks have a less positive reaction to a change in the capital gains tax rate. Their results suggested that holding period, an investor-specific attribute, is a significant variable in explaining the market reaction to a change in the capital gains tax rates.[39]

A 1991 study by Bolster and Vahan found that relative changes in the tax rates on dividends and capital gains affect the market prices of stocks and that the prices of dividend-paying stocks are affected differently than the prices of stocks that do not pay dividends.[40] A later study found that a reduction in future capital gains taxes resulted in increased share prices for nondividend and low-dividend stocks relative to

37 Jia-Wen Liang, Steven R. Matsuanga, and Dale C. Morse, University of Oregon, "The Effect of the Expected Holding Period on the Market Reaction to a Decline in the Capital Gains Tax Rate," *Journal of American Taxation Association*, Winter 2002.

38 Congress of the United States Congressional Budget Office, "How Capital Gains Tax Rates Affect Revenues: The Historical Evidence," A CBO Study, March 1988.

39 Jia-Wen Liang, Steven R. Matsuanga, and Dale C. Morse, University of Oregon, "The Effect of the Expected Holding Period on the Market Reaction to a Decline in the Capital Gains Tax Rate," *Journal of American Taxation Association*, Winter 2002.

40 Paul Bolster and Janigian Vahan, "Dividend Policy and Valuation Effects of the Tax Reform Act of 1986," *National Tax Journal*, December 1991, p. 44.

high-dividend stocks.[41] The authors concluded that capital gains taxes are capitalized into share price; however, they also found that the *anticipation* of tax rate changes leads to a reduction in the market's supply of stock, thus impacting price.[42]

A 2002 study documented that the expected holding period (and thus the deferral of capital gains taxes) is a significant variable in assessing the price reaction to changes in the capital gains tax rate. More specifically, the positive market reaction was lower for dividend-paying and similar securities with longer expected holding periods.[43] Overall, the studies of the capitalization of capital gains tax in price reveal that payout policies, shareholder tax rates, and expected holding period are important considerations.

The shareholder taxes embedded in the market returns used by private-company valuation analysts reflect the payout policies, tax rates, and holding periods of the firms included in the public market proxy (i.e., S&P 500, NYSE, AMEX, and NASDAQ) across the entire time horizon used by the data provider (since 1926 or 1963, depending on what historical return measure the analyst relies upon). It is *this* combined effect we seek to measure when we make an adjustment reflecting the difference between the pass-through entity and the public-market return we use to value it.

The interaction of clienteles, shareholder taxes, and firm value. According to Miller and Modigliani, "the theory of dividend tax clienteles predicts that firms paying little or no dividends will attract investors in higher tax brackets, while firms that pay high dividends will attract investors in lower tax brackets."[44] Tax clienteles affect how firms capitalize shareholder taxes into equity prices. Some studies treat institutional investors as homogeneous tax-exempt groups.[45] Other studies recognize that different tax clienteles exist within institutional investors.[46]

In the public markets, tax clienteles are made up of investors with similar tax attributes. These tax clienteles are naturally drawn to certain investments, much like tax-exempt

41 Mark Lang and Douglas Shackelford, "Capitalization of Capital Gains Taxes: Evidence From Stock Price Reactions to the 1997 Rate Reduction," *Journal of Public Economics*, 2000, 76.

42 David A.Guenther, "Investor Reaction to Anticipated 1997 Capital Gains Tax Rate Reduction," working paper, 1999, Boulder, Colo.: University of Colorado, p. 1.

43 Jia-Wen Liang, Steven R. Matsunaga, and Dale C. Morse, "The Effect of the Expected Holding Period on the Market Reaction to a Decline in the Capital Gains Tax Rate," *Journal of the American Taxation Association*, Winter 2002.

44 William Moser and Andy Puckett, "Dividend Tax Clienteles: Evidence From Tax Law Changes," University of Missouri, 2008, p. 3, citing M. Miller and F. Modigliani, "Dividend Policy, Growth, and the Valuation of Shares," *The Journal of Business*, 1961, 34: 411 433.

45 Dan Dhaliwal, Linda Krull, Oliver Zhen Li, and William Moser, "Dividend Taxes and the Implied Cost of Equity Capital," *Journal of Accounting Research*, December 2005, Vol. 43, No. 5, Elsevier, p. 705.

46 William Moser and Andy Puckett, "Dividend Tax Clienteles: Evidence From Tax Law Changes," University of Missouri, 2008, pp. 3-4.

investors are drawn to fully taxable bonds, while high tax rate investors are drawn to tax-exempt bonds. Just as with the bond example, a specific clientele will logically become the price setter, or marginal investor, for a given equity as investors attempt to maximize after-tax return by matching their tax (and certain nontax) attributes to the expected mix of return from an equity. For example, Erickson and Maydew[47] found that corporations (for which dividend income is tax-favored) are the marginal investors in high-yield stocks. Dhaliwal et al.[48] provide evidence that increases in dividend payouts are associated with increased levels of institutional ownership. Seida also finds evidence consistent with the existence of clienteles on dividend-paying stocks.[49]

Other studies have also found evidence of clienteles related to payout policies and tax effects. Specifically, individuals who hold low dividend-payout stocks tend to pay taxes on those dividends at the ordinary income tax rate. By comparison, "medium" dividend-payout firms are generally owned by tax-free institutions, which pay no tax at all and are indifferent to the relative tax rates on dividends or capital gains. High dividend-paying firms are primarily owned by corporations, which can generally avoid taxation on most of the dividends they receive. Institutional investors prefer dividend-paying stocks, according to one study.[50] Examining the period 1987 to 2004, one study found that, when dividend taxes are high, high dividend-paying firms constitute a large portion of institutions' portfolios and that when dividend taxes decline, institutional ownership in high dividend-paying stocks also decreases.[51]

Of course, one must be careful in drawing certain conclusions as institutional investors may prefer dividends for other, nontax reasons as well. However, as previously discussed, institutional investors with a preference for large, liquid stocks have steadily come to control a growing share of the public market.[52] Total institutional equity holdings represented 28.4% of the total U.S. markets in 1980, rocketing to 50.6% of the total U.S. market by 2009.[53]

47 Merle Erickson and Edward Maydew, "Implicit Taxes in High Dividend Yield Stocks," *Accounting Review*, October 1998, p.73.

48 Dan Dhaliwal, Merle Erickson, Mary Margaret Myers, and Monica Banyi, "Are Shareholder Dividend Taxes on Corporate Retained Earnings Impounded in Equity Prices?: Additional Evidence and Analysis," June 6, 2001, SSRN: ssrn.com/abstract=272663 or DOI: 10.2139/ssrn.272663, p. 16, citing Dan Dhaliwal, Merle Erickson, and Robert Trezevant, "A Test of the Theory of Tax Clienteles for Dividend Policies," *National Tax Journal*, 1999, 52, pp. 179-194.

49 Jim Seida, "Evidence of Tax Clienteles for Common Stock Via the Trading Activity Following Dividend Increases," *Journal of the American Taxation Association*, March 2002.

50 William Moser and Andy Puckett, "Dividend Tax Clienteles: Evidence from Tax Law Changes," University of Missouri, 2008.

51 Ibid., p. 2.

52 Paul A. Gompers, and Andrew Metrick, "Institutional Investors and Equity Prices," *The Quarterly Journal of Economics*, Feb. 1, 2001, Vol. 116, No. 1, p. 231.

53 The Conference Board, *The 2010 Institutional Investment Report, Trends in Institutional Investor Assets and Equity Ownership of U.S. Corporations*, page 22.

Exhibit 4-1 illustrates institutional ownership since 1949.[54]

Exhibit 4-1. Institutional Ownership in the United States, 1949-2013

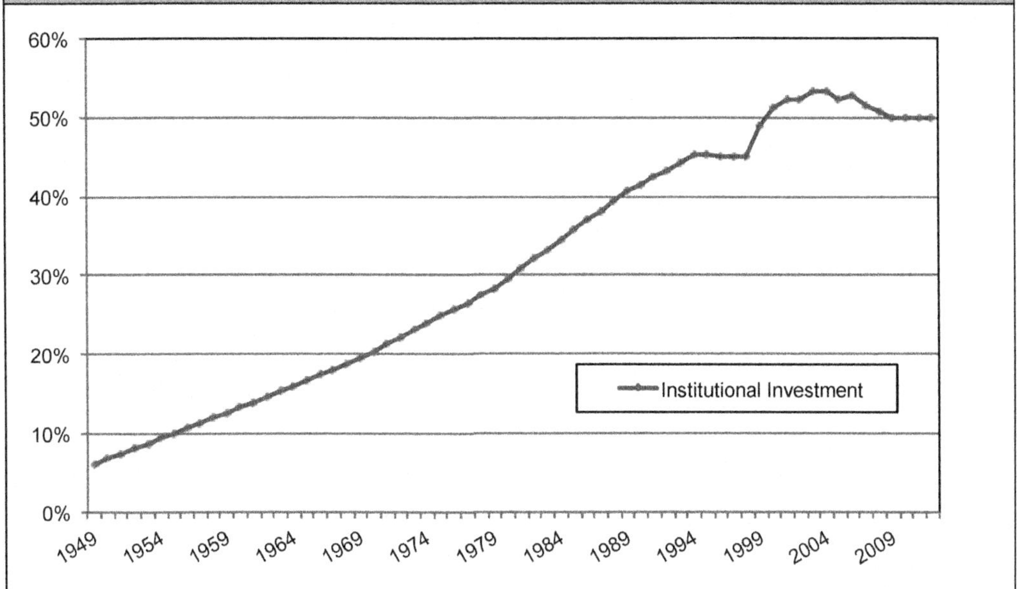

This shift in stock market ownership has had implications for stock prices and returns. One study calculated that the increase in institutional ownership accounted for nearly 50% of the relative price appreciation for large stocks over small stocks during their sample period (1980-1996).[55] This study demonstrated a positive correlation between institutional ownership and firm size. By contrast, a later study concluded that the measure of institutional ownership captures not only a size effect, but also a tax effect.[56] In the years that institutional investors flooded the markets (typically noted as the late 1970s to the present), the "size" effect diminished significantly, as the demand and price of large capitalization stocks increased.

While institutional investors have increased their holdings in the public market overall, the magnitude of investment in small stocks has been rapidly rising. Since 1980, institutional investors have decreased their holdings in large stocks in favor of smaller stocks.[57] The percentage of microcap stocks owned by institutions grew from 11.9% in 1980 to 68.2% in 2010, as institutions displaced individual investors across the entire

54 The Conference Board, *The 2010 Institutional Investment Report, Trends in Institutional Investor Assets and Equity Ownership of U.S. Corporations.*

55 Paul A. Gompers and Andrew Metrick, "Institutional Investors and Equity Prices," *The Quarterly Journal of Economics*, Feb. 1, 2001, Vol. 116, No. 1, p. 231.

56 Dan Dhaliwal, Linda Krull, Oliver Zhen Li, and William Moser, "Dividend Taxes and the Implied Cost of Equity Capital," *Journal of Accounting Research*, December 2005, Vol. 43 No. 5, p. 705.

57 Marshall E. Blume, Donald B. Keim, Howard Butcher III, and John B. Neff, "The Changing Preferences of Institutional Investors for Common Stocks," This Draft, March 11, 2014, p. 1.

public market.[58] However, much of this growth is attributed to hedge funds,[59] which generally pay capital gains taxes on their income. Like individual investors, they further benefit from the ability to defer taxes.[60]

Many studies have noted varying levels of taxes across investors and, in particular, tax-favored institutional investors.[61] Because these institutional investors are frequently tax-exempt, the payment of dividend taxes does not affect them. For example, if the marginal investor of a security is tax-exempt, then investor-level taxes do not affect the price of the security.[62]

Thus, although there is strong evidence that shareholder-level taxes impact firm value, the effect of dividend and capital gains taxes on pricing appears to be muted in the public markets due to the effect of clienteles. For instance, one study found that, from 1962 to 2000, the share of public equities held in retirement accounts and pension funds increased from zero to slightly over 50%.[63] As a result, the authors found that the marginal tax rate on dividends, which was 43% from 1955 to 1962, had dropped to only 17% from 1987 to 2000.[64]

Moreover, some studies suggest that as institutional investment increases they become the marginal, or price-setting, investor.[65] That is, when the institutional investor demands large capitalization, high dividend-paying stocks, they "bid up" the price of these stocks. If other market participants want to hold the same stock, then they have to pay the same price—even if they are subject to a tax effect. Although private-company valuation analysts have sometimes discussed the notion of institutional investors offsetting the tax effect, this generally implies that the taxes have no effect (or at least a greatly diminished effect) when institutional investors are the marginal investor. At the very least, as institutional investor ownership increases, the tax penalty on dividends decreases.

58 Ibid., p. 7.

59 Ibid., "Abstract."

60 Donald J. Marples, "Taxation of Hedge Fund and Private Equity Managers," Congressional Research Service, March 7, 2014.

61 Dan Dhaliwal, Linda Krull, Oliver Zhen Li, and William Moser, "Dividend Taxes and the Implied Cost of Equity Capital," *Journal of Accounting Research*, December 2005, Vol. 43, No. 5, Elsevier, p. 683, citing D. Dhaliwal, M. Erickson, and R. Trezevant, "A Test of the Theory of Tax Clienteles for Dividend Policies," *National Tax Journal* 52, 1999, 179-94; F. Allen, A. Bernardo, and I. Welch, "A Theory of Dividends Based on Tax Clienteles," *Journal of Finance*, 2000, 55, 2499-556; M. Miller, and M. Scholes, "Dividends and Taxes, Some Empirical Evidence," *Journal of Political Economy*, 90 (1982), 1118-41.

62 Jia-Wen Liang, Steven R. Matsunaga,, and Dale C. Morse, "The Effect of the Expected Holding Period on the Market Reaction to a Decline in the Capital Gains Tax Rate," *Journal of the American Taxation Association*, Winter 2002.

63 Rajnish Mehra and Edward Prescott, "The Equity Premium in Retrospect," NBER Working Paper No. 9525, NBER, March 2003. See also Mehra and Prescott, "The Equity Premium in Retrospect," *Guide of the Economics of Finance*, Ch. 14 (Elsvier B.V. 2003).

64 Ibid.

65 Richard W. Sias and Laura T. Starks, "Return Autocorrelation and Institutional Investors," *Journal of Financial Economics*, 1997, 46, p. 104.

One study investigated the impact of tax-exempt investors and the relation between investor-level taxes and value.[66] The authors found that investors shift their portfolios if and when different types of income are taxed at different rates. Unlike an earlier study,[67] this one concluded that "tax-exempt investors drive down the dividend tax penalty for every stock."[68] This research differs from the prior studies in at least one important respect, as the authors observe:

> The level of tax-exempt investor ownership of any particular firm should have no effect on the dividend tax penalty. Therefore, tax-exempt investors do mitigate the dividend tax penalty but not in the manner suggested by prior empirical tax papers in accounting. The dividend tax penalty is the same for all firms with the same dividend yield, regardless of the level of tax-exempt ownership in any particular firm.[69]

This is important for our discussion of the market return because it has embedded in it the effect of institutional investors across all stocks.

Having reviewed the research, we now turn to the implications of it to private-company valuation.

66 David A. Guenther and Richard Sansing, "The Effect of Tax-Exempt Investors on Stock Ownership and the Dividend Tax Penalty," October 2007. www.kellogg.northwestern.edu/accounting/papers/Sansing.doc.

67 Dan Dhaliwal, Linda Krull, Oliver Zhen Li and William Moser, "Dividend Taxes and the Implied Cost of Equity Capital," *Journal of Accounting Research* (Blackwell), December 2005, Vol. 43 No. 5.

68 David A. Guenther and Richard Sansing, "The Effect of Tax-Exempt Investors on Stock Ownership and the Dividend Tax Penalty," October 2007. www.kellogg.northwestern.edu/accounting/papers/Sansing.doc.

69 Ibid., p. 3.

Chapter 5. Impact of Prior Research on Private-Company Valuation

The prior chapter reviewed the relevant research pertaining to the impact of shareholder-level taxes on stock prices and returns observed in the public equity markets. Prior research conclusively demonstrates that shareholder-level taxes can impact equity value. Given this, it appears that appraisers attempting to determine the value of a pass-through entity have two choices:

1. On the one hand, they can attempt to remove the effects of shareholder-level taxes that are embedded in observed market returns, yielding a return that reflects only entity-level taxes. Such a return would be suitable for estimating the value of projected earnings that have been reduced by entity-specific taxes but not shareholder taxes.

2. Alternatively, they can use unadjusted market returns, which, as we have demonstrated, impound certain shareholder-level tax and nontax attributes. To use this measure, the appraiser would need to either adjust the income stream against which the unadjusted return is applied or adjust the value determination with a premium or discount, so that the result yields the appropriate value.

Both alternatives emphasize the importance of matching the selected cash-flow measure with the appropriate cost of capital. Exhibit 5-1 demonstrates that, regardless of which alternative the analyst uses, the resulting valuation will be the same.

Exhibit 5-1. Matching of Cash Flows to Cost of Capital (Statutory Rates)

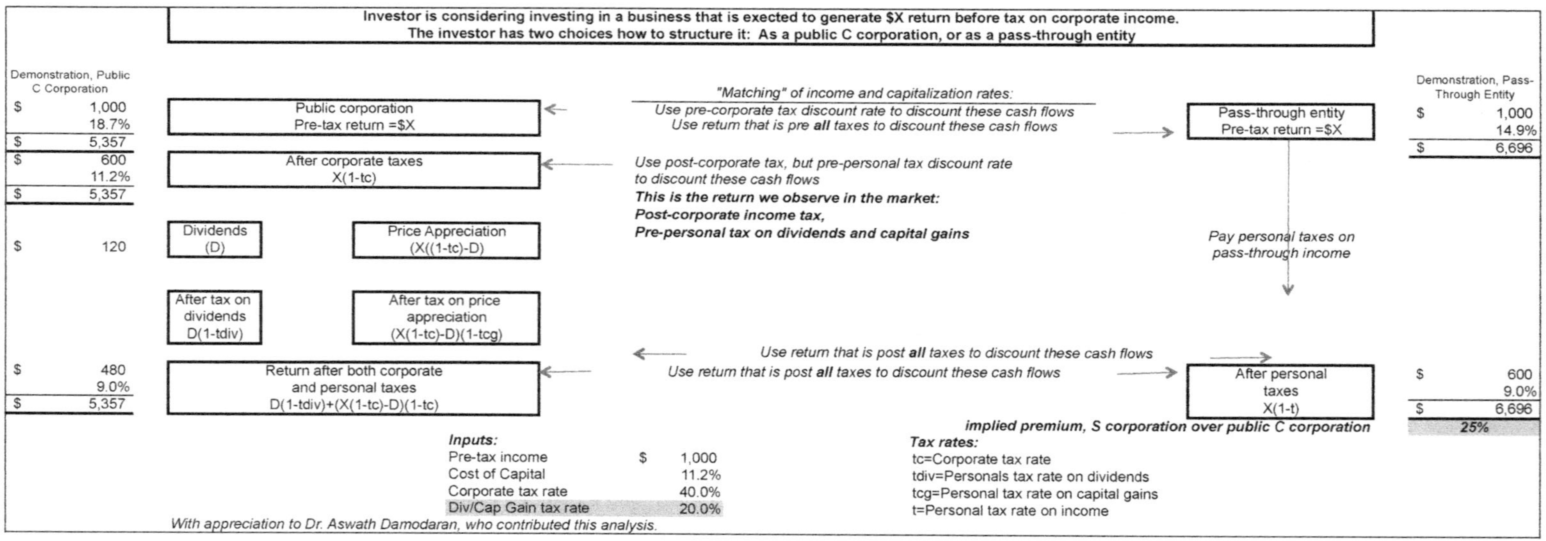

Exhibit 5-1 demonstrates the long-accepted view that cash flows should be matched with a cost of capital that has the same tax attributes.

Using either approach presents challenges. In either case, the appraiser must identify and quantify the effects of shareholder-level taxes, either to remove them entirely from the cost of capital estimate or to properly match them to the income stream used to value the private company. However, the market return was developed over a long time horizon and includes the effects of varying tax rates, holding periods, and clienteles. As such, this involves far more than simply "backing out" or adjusting for current statutory tax rates.

The research demonstrates that company-specific and shareholder-specific attributes play a significant part in determining the magnitude of the impact of shareholder-level taxes on the cost of equity of public companies. Not only do these attributes vary across firms, but they also have varied significantly over time and, most critically, are frequently unobservable. Moreover, several of these company-specific and shareholder-specific attributes *interact*, and that interaction takes place in a market where companies are free to adjust their payout strategies and investors are free to constantly re-evaluate and reposition their investment decisions based on current, actual, and anticipated changes in their individual tax situation, overall tax regimes, cash-flow needs, and changes in corporate dividend policy.

Because of these changes, the observed long-horizon equity risk premium currently relied upon by business appraisers is estimated using an amalgam of companies with varying payout policies (not only among firms, but also across time) combined with the expectations of many and varied investors.[70] In summary, many issues and attributes affect the presence and magnitude of shareholder taxes and their effect on value. To this point in our analysis, we can refine these issues and state them as follows:

1. Actual and anticipated shareholder-level taxes are capitalized in market price and, by extension, in observed market returns;
2. Market participants (individuals, institutions, etc.) and their tax situations affect the magnitude of firms' tax capitalization;
3. The composition of market participants and tax clienteles has changed over time;
4. Firms respond to changing tax policies by attempting to minimize shareholder taxes;

70 Each of the expert witnesses in the *Gross v. Commissioner* case relied upon Morningstar data, which captures returns in the U.S. equity markets since the 1920s.

5. Investors also respond to tax policies by maximizing after-shareholder-level returns; and

6. Changes in any of these factors can change the marginal investor for a given security.

Despite the challenges presented by this dynamic market, and in fact thanks to it, research has also been able to determine that the impact of shareholder-level taxes on public-market prices is lessened by a combination of rational, after-tax, return-maximizing behavior on the part of investor clienteles and similar cost of equity capital-minimizing behavior by companies.

When a required rate of return metric derived from historical market returns is used to value a private company, analysts need to understand the characteristics of that public return data and use care when selecting appropriate data so that the data will best match the characteristics of the subject company. That is, they need to ensure that the cost of capital matches the measure of cash flow used in the valuation. This need to "match" the return with the cash flow is true for every valuation.

How is this matching possible, given the amalgam of factors impounded in market returns? In the following chapters, we discuss the existing alternatives and propose a possible alternative solution, which, like the problems, has been identified largely through empirical research.

Chapter 6. Foundation for Cash Flow-Based Models

This chapter presents the foundation for the S corp models, the Delaware Chancery model, and the no tax affect model (collectively, the "cash flow-based models").[71] The foundation for these models is straightforward in application and can be incorporated into any capitalization or discounting calculation. Once analysts understand the foundation, the application in any valuation is a facts-and-circumstances determination of the extent to which shareholder taxes for the subject company are preferential over the public market, including consideration of offsetting detriments.

Review of existing cash flow-based models. Recall from Chapter 1 that the no tax affect model (such as that adopted by the Tax Court) represents an assumption that taxes borne at the shareholder level do not affect value and, accordingly, should be ignored when valuing a pass-through entity. Such reasoning leads to a premium for the pass-through entity of as much as 67%, as was demonstrated in Exhibit 1-4.

Clearly, investors in double-taxed entities would be elated to learn that, by simply making a tax election (i.e., by electing to file as a subchapter S corporation), they could increase the value of their company by 67%! Unfortunately for such investors, however, this is not the case. Recognizing this, most valuation analysts who would choose to ignore the effect of personal taxes on value would make some other (equally unsupported) offsetting adjustments to counter this irrational effect. (In fact, some valuation analysts have done just this, by advocating taking a larger discount for lack of marketability to offset the overstated adjustment determined by the no tax affect model. The old adage, "two wrongs do not make a right," applies here.)

71 This guide does not present or advocate for any particular cash flow-based model.

As noted earlier, several private-company valuation professionals reacted to the decisions of the U.S. Tax Court by designing models that recognized that, while pass-through entity investors do not avoid taxes on corporate income, compared to their publicly traded counterparts, they do avoid dividend and capital gains taxes. On the surface, the most widely used S corp models appear to be very different from each other. However, at their core, they all do the same thing: recognize the benefit of avoiding the potential double tax on dividends and capital gains.

The underlying foundation of the S corp models is simple, as presented in Exhibit 6-1.

Exhibit 6-1. Foundation for S Corp Models

	Public C Corp	S Corp
Income before corporate tax	$100	$100
Corporate income tax rate	40%	0%
Available earnings	$60	$100
Taxes at personal level	20%	40%
Available after taxes at personal level	$48	$60
"Premium" per S corporation models		**25%**

The S corp models recognize that taxes on corporate income impact the cash flow that is available for distribution or growth in both publicly traded C corporations and pass-through entities. However (as the theory goes), only the publicly traded C corporation investors in this comparative analysis pay shareholder (dividend and capital gains) tax. Therefore, there must be a relative benefit to owning an S corporation, measured by the avoidance of these taxes. As such, in the application of the income approach, an adjustment to the value of the pass-through entity is made by comparison of it to that which is embedded in the public-market return.[72]

The S corp models (whichever one the analyst uses) represent a huge step forward, taking into account the fact that personal taxes matter to investors and affect value. A 2006 decision by the Delaware Chancery Court[73] recognized the work that the valuation profession had done in creating the S corp models and agreed that the benefit of pass-through entity status was in the avoidance of personal (dividend and capital gains) taxes. Referencing the work Chris Treharne and Chris Mercer did, the Delaware

72 As noted in Chapter 1, as analysts do not calculate other methods of valuation (such as the transaction method and net asset approach) by reference to public-market returns with embedded taxes (as in their development of the income approach and guideline company method), one would not make similar tax adjustments to these other methods. Other methods of valuation may have other tax issues; however, these tax issues would be separate and distinct from those discussed in this text and would require wholly separate considerations, including any benefit that might be obtained from a 338(h)(10) election.

73 *Delaware Open MRI Radiology Associates, P.A. v. Kessler*, CA-275-N, 2006 Del. Ch. LEXIS 84 (2006).

Chancery derived its own model[74] as shown in Exhibit 6-2.

Exhibit 6-2. Pass-Through Entity Valuation Model Employed by the Delaware Chancery Court

	Publicly Traced C Corp Proxy	S Corp	Tax Rate Used in S Corporation Valuation	"Premium" or ("Detriment")
Income before tax	$100	$100	$100	
Tax rate on corporate income	40%	0.0%	**28.00%**	
Available earnings	$60	$100	$72	
Dividend or personal income tax rate	20%	40%	20%	
Available after dividend	$48	$60	$60	**25.0%**
"Premuim" or ("detriment")		**25.0%**		

The Delaware Chancery accomplishes the same thing that was at the core of each of the S corp models, that is, compare the attributes of the public-market return (and the assumed cash flow that would be available to a public C corporation investor) to that which would be available to a pass-through entity investor.

A critical assumption both the S corp models and the Delaware Chancery model make is that both public-market investors (whose attributes are reflected in the market return) and S corporation investors paid taxes at *statutory rates*. With this assumption, the differences in taxes result in an S corporation premium. In the Delaware Chancery model, this premium was added to the S corporation by effectively "plugging" a reduced rate of taxes on corporate earnings. However, regardless of whether the analyst uses the Delaware Chancery model or any one of the S corp models, the magnitude of the premium (assuming the same inputs) are materially (if not exactly) the same.

74 There have been some attempts to discredit the widely used "Delaware Chancery" model, which the Delaware Chancery Court originally employed in a 2006 case. However, the Delaware Chancery model is virtually the same model as the no tax affect model, if one were to use the same inputs. This is demonstrated below:

	Public C Corp	S Corp	S-Corp Valuation
Income before corporate tax	$100	$100	$100
Corporate income tax rate	40%	0%	0%
Available earnings	$60	$100	$100
Taxes at personal level	0%	0%	0%
Available after taxes at personal level	$60	$100	$100
"Premium"			**67%**

Up until now, methods of accounting for the effect of shareholder taxes on value calculated the taxes presumed to be embedded in the cost of capital *assuming that public C corporations' investors pay taxes at statutory rates.* As the research demonstrates, this assumption is false. When using public-market returns as calculated by commercially available sources (i.e., Duff & Phelps), the analyst is using a rate with effective shareholder taxes embedded in it; to the extent it captures a tax effect on value that does not exist in the pass-through entity, it is *this effect* that needs to be adjusted.[75]

Adjusting the cash flow-based models to more appropriately account for embedded taxes. While the cash flow-based models accomplished a great deal, they proved to be naïve in one critical respect. Specifically, they did not examine a key, underlying assumption that they all had in common: the assumption that the historical public-market return includes the effect of all investors in the public marketplace paying dividend and capital gains taxes immediately and at statutory rates.

Herein lies the crux of the issue: The S corp models and the Delaware Chancery model assume that all investors in the public-market proxy (generally, either the S&P 500 or NYSE/NASDAQ/AMEX) actually pay the statutory dividend and capital gains tax rates. As discussed, the research demonstrates that this assumption is false. All investors seek to minimize, defer, or avoid taxes. Further, a significant slice of the public market is held by institutional investors, the majority of whom pay no tax at all, thereby muting to some degree the effect of any taxes included therein.

This logically leads to the conclusion that any premium ascribed to a pass-through entity should be lower than the 25% maximum calculated as if no mitigating factors existed.

One way the analyst can consider reflecting this in the S corp models is by employing a lower dividend tax rate (to account for the fact that not all investors pay such taxes). We demonstrate this in Exhibit 6-3 by use of the model employed by the Delaware Chancery Court:[76]

75 It is also true that shareholders in the private market experience taxes that are not experienced by public-market investors. These taxes are a "penalty" relative to the public market return and should be taken into account.

76 The focus of this guide is the effect of dividend and capital gains taxes on public-market returns and the implications for private-company valuation. Analysts employing the cash flow-based models also need to consider the magnitude of the taxes on corporate income deducted in their analyses. As to the pass-through entity's taxes on corporate income, the analyst will likely want to use the same rate of tax that he or she felt reasonable in the determination of the pass-through entity's net cash flow. As to the publicly traded C corporation proxy, the amount of corporate tax should reflect that which is embedded in the long-horizon public-market return. We have identified this latter tax as an area for further research in Appendix A. At this time, we are aware that most analysts assume that the two corporate tax burdens are of a similar magnitude.

Exhibit 6-3. Illustration of Muted Tax Affect: Pass-Through Entity Valuation Model Employed by the Delaware Chancery Court, Modified for Muted Effect of Embedded Taxes in Market Return

	Publicly Traced C Corp Proxy	S Corp	Tax Rate Used in S Corporation Valuation	"Premium" or ("Detriment")
Income before tax	$100	$100	$100	
Tax rate on corporate income	40%	0.0%	**34.00%**	
Available earnings	$60	$100	$66	
Dividend or personal income tax rate	10%	40%	10%	
Available after dividend	$54	$60	$60	**11.1%**
"Premuim" or ("detriment")		**11.1%**		

Reducing the embedded dividend and capital gains tax rate used in the analysis, for all the reasons discussed in this guide, results in a decrease in the implied "premium" for the pass-through entity. In the example above, we have applied an effective dividend tax rate of 10% for illustrative purposes.

But how do you decide what dividend/capital gains tax rate to employ? We examine that question in the next section.

Dividend and/or capital gains taxes borne by public market investors. The shareholder (dividend and capital gains) taxes deducted from the cash flow-based models should reflect the fact that public-market investors pay a mix of dividend and capital gains taxes (the latter of which may be deferred), and many investors pay no tax at all. Therefore, the extent of shareholder taxes deducted from the public-market C corporation component of the calculation should be muted.

In determining the magnitude of the dividend taxes to be deducted in the cash flow-based models, consider, for example, that Dhaliwal's research indicated that the presence of institutional investors reduced the dividend tax premium by over 57% as of 2005; if nothing else, this, alone, should tell analysts that the shareholder tax embedded in the market return is less than the statutory rate. Other factors, including other clientele effects and tax deferral opportunities, would lead to the embedded taxes being even less. Thus, from a "50,000-foot view," research informs us that using the statutory rate in any of the S corp models almost certainly overstates the magnitude of the calculated premium.

One way to make a more specific determination of how much to mute the market return is to consider:

1. The mix of dividend and capital gains tax embedded in the market return;
2. The long-horizon effective dividend tax rates borne on the income return component;
3. The long-horizon effective capital gains tax rates borne on the capital gain component, taking into consideration that these taxes should reflect opportunities to defer such taxes.

The following provides an example using historical returns as typically calculated by the data providers used by most private-company valuation analysts. Such returns are after corporate income tax and incorporate the effects of shareholder taxes. Assume that, of the total return, the long-horizon income return was 4.1%, and the long-horizon capital gains tax return was 6.9%. This would mean that the income return represented approximately 37% of the total return, and the capital gain return represented approximately 63%. Further, assume:

- A total return of $1,000;
- A long-horizon effective dividend tax rate of 20.6% (federal and state combined);
- A long-horizon effective capital gains tax rate of 16.0% (federal and state combined);
- A long-horizon tax-preferred institutional investment in the public market proxy of 16.5%;
- The long-horizon average holding period in the market is 3.8 years; and
- The total return (used to estimate the present value of the capital gains tax affect) is 11%.

Using these assumptions, the amount of embedded shareholder tax is then calculated as shown in Exhibit 6-4.

Each of these components for the returns most commonly used by valuation analysts (arithmetic average income and capital gain returns, arithmetic average low-or-no taxed institutional investors, and arithmetic average holding period) can be found in Chapter 8.

Exhibit 6-4. Demonstration of Calculation of Shareholder Tax Embedded in Public-Market Return

	Income	Capital Gain	Total Tax	Total Return
Return component (arithmetic average)	$369	$631		$1,000
Effective tax rate (arithmetic average)	20.6%	16.0%		
1 minus tax-favored institutional investment	84.0%	84.0%		
Tax on income return component			$64	
Tax on capital gain component		$85		
Holding period (arithmentic average)		3.8		
Present-value rate (total return, as reinvestment rate)		11.0%		
Present-value, tax on capital gain			$57	$121
Shareholder tax on observed market return				**12.1%**

Using the cash flow-based models, this would result in a premium calculated as shown in Exhibit 6-5.

Exhibit 6-5. Illustrative Calculation of Pass-Through Entity 'Premium' Using Shareholder Tax on Observed Market Returns

	Public C Corp	S Corp
Income before corporate tax	$100	$100
Corporate income tax rate	40%	0%
Available earnings	$60	$100
Taxes at personal level	12.1%	40%
Available after taxes at personal level	$53	$60
"Premium"		**13.8%**

Note that, while this calculation takes into account many of the considerations that would serve to mute any shareholder tax penalty, it does not fully account for clientele effects, that is, stocks that yield the lowest dividends attract investors in the higher tax brackets, and high dividend-yield stocks attract investors in lower tax brackets.[77] Studies further suggest that investors could escape the dividend tax penalty altogether by levering their purchases of equities, offsetting taxable dividends with interest deductions.[78] These factors, which are unobservable or, at the very least, extremely difficult to measure (particularly over a long time horizon), would serve to further mitigate the tax effect of dividends in the equity rate.

77 Dan Dhaliwal, Linda Krull, Oliver Zhen Li, and William Moser, "Dividend Taxes and the Implied Cost of Equity Capital," *Journal of Accounting Research*, December 2005, Vol. 43, No. 5, p. 680.

78 Miller and Scholes (1979); Robert H. Litzenberger and Krishna Ramaswamy, "Dividends, Short Selling Restrictions, Tax-Induced Investor Clienteles and Market Equilibrium," *The Journal of Finance*, May 1980, Vol. 35, No. 2 , p. 470.

Summary. This chapter reviewed the foundation for the cash flow-based models, with particular focus on the assumptions analysts have typically made in their application, compared to what research tells us.

An alternative to the cash flow-based models is to make an adjustment directly to the cost of capital, where the mismatch arises in the first place. Our analysis of the manner of making an adjustment begins with the research related to the magnitude of taxes that are embedded in the cost of capital.

Chapter 7. Research Related to the Magnitude of Taxes Embedded in the Cost of Capital

Perhaps the most intuitive approach to removing the embedded effects of shareholder-level taxes is similar to the approach by which analysts value riskless (or nearly riskless) taxable versus tax-exempt bonds. In the case of riskless bonds, investors are indifferent to owning taxable or tax-exempt bonds as long as the after-tax yield to them is the same. Typically, investors in high-tax brackets will hold tax-exempt bonds and investors in low-tax brackets will hold taxable bonds. Unfortunately, although this theory holds for riskless or low-risk securities, firms in the public market are not "otherwise identical" to a private company.[79]

Guenther and Sansing find that "sorting" evidence in riskless assets is not the same as evidenced in the larger stock market, where investors form clienteles based not only on tax considerations, but also on their tolerance for risk. "Tax considerations, however, induce investors to adjust their portfolios, but not to the corner solution found in the case of riskless bonds."[80]

Thus, although individuals generally hold low dividend-paying stocks and institutions hold high dividend-paying stocks, "[r]isk-sharing considerations mitigate the effects of investor-level taxation on portfolio choice. In turn, this causes stock returns to reflect the tax characteristics of *all investors*, as opposed to the tax rate of a hypothetical marginal

79 While private-company valuation analysts widely acknowledge the fact that firms in the public market are not "otherwise identical" to private companies, it has not prevented general acceptance among practitioners of public-market returns (adjusted for size, illiquidity, etc.) as the foundation for the income approach.

80 David A. Guenther and Richard Sansing, "The Effect of Tax-Exempt Investors on Stock Ownership and the Dividend Tax Penalty," October 2007, p. 5. www.kellogg.northwestern.edu/accounting/papers/Sansing.doc.

investor."[81] Further, in using the market return, we are adopting the taxes embedded in it; these are the taxes that we must identify and, to the extent an investor in the private market will not experience them, remove.

Dhaliwal et al. used statistical measures to test for the effect of taxes on the cost of capital. They pose and examine two hypotheses:

- H1: "The relation between the implied cost of equity capital and dividend yield is increasing in the magnitude of the dividend tax penalty"; and
- H2: "The positive relation between the implied cost of equity capital and the tax-penalized portion of dividend yield is decreasing in the aggregate level of institutional ownership."[82]

In other words, the researchers first examine the relationship between dividend yield and the firm's cost of equity capital. Next, they examine the impact that institutional ownership has on this relationship. To test their hypotheses, Dhaliwal et al. construct a cross-sectional, time series regression model using an annual (time series) measure of the implied equity risk premium for a large number of publicly traded firms as the dependent variable.[83] Independent (explanatory) variables include the tax-penalized portion of dividend yield for each firm, the level of institutional ownership for each firm, and the interaction of these two variables. They also control for other factors by including the ratio of book-to-market value of equity, growth, and other industry- and company-specific risk factors. By examining the statistical significance, magnitude, and sign of the regression coefficients pertaining to each variable, they measure the impact of shareholder-level dividend taxes and institutional ownership on company-specific cost of capital.[84]

Dhaliwal et al. explain their hypotheses as follows:

> H1 suggests that the implied cost of equity capital is increasing in the tax penalized portion of dividend yield. If the dividend tax penalty is capitalized into stock price, then the relation between dividend yield and cost of equity capital should increase

81 David A. Guenther and Richard Sansing, "The Effect of Tax-Exempt Investors on Stock Ownership and the Dividend Tax Penalty," October 2007, p. 5. (emphasis added) www.kellogg.northwestern.edu/accounting/papers/Sansing.doc.

82 Dan Dhaliwal, Linda Krull, Oliver Zhen Li, and William Moser, "Dividend Taxes and the Implied Cost of Equity Capital," *Journal of Accounting Research*, December 2005, Vol. 43 No. 5, p. 683.

83 Implied cost of equity measures are forward-looking measures that do not rely on the same mix of returns and tax regimes encountered when using historical returns to estimate cost of equity.

84 The Dhaliwal et al. study incorporated all public companies data from 1980 to 2001 for which complete data were available. Depending on the estimate of implied cost of capital used, the number of observations used in the regression ranged from 18,416 firm-years to 16,200 firm-years.

> in the magnitude of the dividend tax penalty. Thus, we expect the coefficient on $yield_{i,t-1} \cdot penalty_{i,t}$ to be positive. H2 suggests that the positive effect of $yield_{i,t-1} \cdot penalty_{i,t}$ should decrease in the level of aggregate institutional ownership. Therefore, we expect the coefficient on $yield_{i,t-1} \cdot penalty_{i,t} \cdot inst_{i,t}$ to be negative.[85]

Consistent with their hypotheses, Dhaliwal et al. find a positive relationship between cost of capital and tax penalty. Finding that the "dividend tax effect is an important component of a firm's cost of equity capital,"[86] overall, the regression analysis was used to explain the extent that the equity risk premium (ERP) was affected by shareholder taxes, providing confirming evidence that higher levels of dividend taxation is capitalized into common stock returns and that the magnitude of the tax capitalization is a function of the marginal investor's tax attributes.[87] Regression analysis demonstrated a relationship between the ex ante measures of cost of capital used in their analysis and the tax penalty of approximately 0.4 to 0.5.[88] Notably, this finding is not an absolute tax penalty. Rather, it is the tax penalty arising from the higher rate on dividends than capital gains. Removing this penalty from the cost of equity capital will result in a cost of capital as if dividends were taxed at the same (lower) rate as capital gains. Thus, even after this adjustment, there would still be a tax penalty embedded in the cost of capital.

The impact of the tax penalty was calculated by multiplying the regression coefficient by the amount of the dividend tax penalty (dividend times tax penalty rate). That is, they multiplied:

Regression coefficient × percent income return × tax rate[89]

The researchers concluded that the shareholder tax had increased the ERP by the result and that, had the taxes not been present, the ERP would have been lower.[90] This ERP is measured using observed returns. However, the observed returns that analysts have historically used are not the final return to shareholders. After they pay their dividend and capital gains taxes, their final returns are smaller. Using this final measure of return (after shareholder-level taxes) would result in a lower estimated ERP. To offset these taxes, share prices are reduced, which increases observed (and actual) returns. The researchers further found that, "while tax-penalized dividends increase the cost

85 Dan Dhaliwal, Linda Krull, Oliver Zhen Li, and William Moser, "Dividend Taxes and the Implied Cost of Equity Capital," *Journal of Accounting Research*, December 2005, Vol. 43 No. 5, p. 687.
86 Ibid., p. 697.
87 Ibid., p. 677.
88 Ibid., p. 697.
89 Ibid., p. 698.
90 Ibid., p. 697.

of equity capital, tax advantaged marginal investors reduce the positive correlation."[91] Specifically, they found that the presence of institutional owners reduces the dividend tax premium by 57.21%.[92]

The calculated amount was the amount believed to *increase the implied equity risk premium*, as a result of the shareholder tax penalty. Thus, to remove the effect of shareholder taxes, it should be subtracted from the market return.[93]

Implications of research. For the courts, the IRS, and analysts in the private-capital markets, this is perhaps the bottom line: Extensive research on the public-market return demonstrates that shareholder taxes do not affect company value as if such taxes were paid at the statutory rate (as the cash flow-based models presume), and, in fact, researchers have spent decades and still report that the quantification of *any* tax capitalization is "mixed and controversial." Where private-market valuation today treats shareholder taxes as if they were paid at statutory rates and were directly correlated to value, such treatment is a leap from that which empirical research demonstrates. At the very least, this should indicate to private-market analysts the need to carefully consider the magnitude of the adjustment that needs to be made to properly match the cost of capital with the pass-through entity's income.

Having reviewed the manner in which the magnitude of tax capitalization was tested in academic research studies, we now turn to the application of such research in an alternative to the cash flow-based models.

91 Ibid., p. 696.

92 Ibid., p. 697.

93 Readers should be cautioned that the purpose of Dhaliwal et al. was not to develop a company-specific equity risk premium. Rather, their study was basic research designed to further our understanding of the relationship between taxes and market returns. However, their model and conclusions certainly suggest a possible solution to the issues raised in this guide.

Chapter 8. An Alternative Approach to the Valuation of Pass-Through Entities

Valuation analysts have typically made their adjustment for tax effects as a cash-flow adjustment, in the manner described in Chapter 6. However, as the rate of return we derive from the public marketplace reflects the effects of shareholder taxes on value, one may conclude that the place to make any adjustment for taxes is to the discount rate itself, to remove the effect of embedded shareholder-level taxes. This is a more direct way of valuing the pass-through entity than the cash flow-based models as it adjusts the cost of capital so that it "matches" the subject company's cash flows.

Accordingly, in this chapter, we combine the information from the academic studies together with empirical data from public-market returns and demonstrate how the analyst might use the combined information to more accurately measure cost of capital and firm value. We caution that this research is ongoing and more research needs to be done (see Appendix A, "Suggested Areas for Further Research"). However, where the cash flow-based models largely relied on hypothesis and conjecture, application of those models can now consider the evidence provided by peer-reviewed, scientific research relating to the effects of shareholder taxes on firm values and returns.

A direct approach to valuing the pass-through entity. As this guide has discussed extensively, it is imperative that the cost of capital be properly matched with the cash flows. A valuation of any company using the income approach has two components: a measure of cash flow and a cost of capital. For the direct valuation of a pass-through entity, these components are:

- Net cash flow available to the pass-through entity investor, after payment of combined federal, state, and local taxes due on pass-through earnings, using effective tax rates of the actual or hypothetical investor (actual, if an investment valuation, or value-to-the-holder, analysis is being performed, and hypothetical, if a fair market value analysis is being performed); and
- The discount rate, from which the embedded effect of dividend and capital gains taxes, as inferred by academic research, has been removed.

The *Gross* case says: "If … the discount rate is assumed to be an after-shareholder-tax rate of return, *then the cash-flow should be reduced ('tax affected') to an after-shareholder-tax amount*." (Emphasis added)

We agree wholeheartedly with this statement; academic research clearly demonstrates that shareholder dividend and capital gains taxes affect the cost of capital. Stock prices are reduced (and, therefore, the return derived from it is higher than it would otherwise be) because investors have to pay personal taxes. However, if all we had to consider was personal taxes, S corporations would be worth *far less* than a comparable public C corporation; this is because public-market investors pay personal taxes (assuming statutory rates) on the order of magnitude of 20% of dividends and capital gains, while S corporation shareholders pay taxes at the personal level on the order of magnitude of 40% of flow-through income.

However, not only do shareholder taxes affect value, our basic value calculation demonstrates that *all taxes matter*. As shown in Chapter 3, Equation 1:

Equity Valuation Model

$$Ve = \sum_{t=0}^{\infty} \frac{CFe_t}{(1+r)^t} \cdots > 0$$

where:

Ve = the value of equity;

CFe_t = the expected net (after tax) cash flows to equity during period t; and

r = the investor/shareholder's required after-tax rate of return.

The tax court agreed that all taxes matter in *Estate of Gallagher v. Commissioner*, when it said that the "principal benefit enjoyed by S corporation shareholders is the *reduction of their total tax burden*."[94] It is this "total tax burden" of the public C corporation compared to the "total tax burden" of the S corporation that we seek to address in the valuation of an S corporation so that we can ensure we have a proper matching of the cost of capital derived from the public market to the S corporation.

94 *Estate of Gallagher v. Commissioner*, T.C. Memo 2011-148.

How do these tax burdens compare?

- *First level of tax:*
    - The first level of tax on the income of a public C corporation is income tax.
    - The first level of tax on the income of a pass-through entity is income tax, borne at the shareholder level.
    - *We generally assume that these taxes are of an order of magnitude that is similar.*
- *Second level of tax:*
    - The second level of tax on the income of a public C corporation is taxes on dividends and capital gains; *these taxes are capitalized into public stock market pricing.*
    - Pass-through entity owners do not pay taxes on dividends or capital gains.

It is *this mismatch* between our cost of capital derived from the public markets and the S corporation that we seek to address.

The two valuation components, in which we address this mismatch between net cash flow and the discount rate, will be discussed in the next sections.

Net cash flow available to pass-through entity investor. This guide has extensively discussed the fact that all taxes affect value. In particular, it has focused on the research demonstrating that shareholder taxes have a negative effect on stock price. Clearly, investors evaluate their shareholder-level taxes when selecting and pricing stocks of public companies. Some analysts (following positions held by the Tax Court and the IRS) have not deducted taxes on corporate income from the S corporation income stream, citing the fact that the corporation itself bears no income tax, and, therefore, any taxes borne at the shareholder level have no effect on value. The research presented herein strongly refutes this position.

Clearly, if taxes borne at the shareholder level at a (current) maximum statutory rate of 20% negatively affect public stock market price, then taxes borne at the shareholder level by pass-through entity investors also affect value. Although the impact of such taxes are muted in the public market (by the presence of institutional investors and deferral opportunities), no similar opportunity to avoid taxes exists for pass-through entity investors. Therefore, these taxes on corporate income should be deducted in the development of the cash-flow stream.

Framework for adjusting the discount rate for effects of embedded taxes. In the approach to valuing pass-through entities that we propose, the cash flow is expressed after the payment of taxes on corporate income. Pass-through entity investors do not further pay dividend and capital gains tax. However, the historical public-market return has embedded in it the effects of dividend and capital gains taxes borne by public-market investors. Market prices reflect the penalty shareholders bear for future shareholder-level taxes on both dividends and capital gains. To match the cost of capital to the pass-through entity income stream, analysts need to remove these embedded tax effects. To revisit what the research has shown, the fact that investors have to pay dividend and capital gains tax negatively affects public stock market prices. If stock price is negatively affected, then the rate of return derived from it is higher than it would otherwise be if investors did not have to pay such taxes. Therefore, the magnitude of the embedded dividend and capital gains tax should be removed, when the cost of capital is being used to value a company whose investors will not bear such taxes.

But how much needs to be removed? As discussed in this guide, various researchers have studied the magnitude of personal taxes impounded in equity returns. However, these studies are not of the same time horizon as the historical returns business valuation analysts most commonly use.

The time horizon over which the tax effect is measured is critical. Analysts regularly acknowledge the importance of this when they make a size adjustment to their cost of capital. The calculation of the size adjustment is made over the same time horizon that the equity risk premium is calculated. Just as the period of measurement of the effect of size on value that analysts commonly use is the same as the period over which the market return is developed, so, too, does the term over which the effects of tax capitalization is measured need to be the same as the period over which the market return is developed. For most analysts, this is either 1926 to the present or 1963 to the present (if using Duff & Phelps' *Valuation Handbook*).

Although the academic research cited in this guide did not use the same time horizon as the historical returns most analysts use, by using the logic and methodology of the Dhaliwal study, analysts can make a similar calculation for the relevant time horizon of their selected return. Such estimation requires a calculation of the tax penalty embedded in the historical return from either 1926 or 1963 to the present. In the following section, we present our calculations based on the data available to us at this time. We fully acknowledge that these calculations incorporate various assumptions and hope to verify and/or improve upon them over time as more research is done (see Appendix A). However, we believe the ability to rely on the results of rigorous research, empirical data, and reasonable estimates represents a significant improvement over the currently used, theoretical methods.

Calculating the adjustment. The tax penalty can be estimated by calculating the shareholder taxes borne by public-market investors over the return horizon.[95,96] Investors in the public market earn a combination of income and capital gain returns. The returns that analysts use are comprised of an arithmetic average of income returns (over either 1926 to the present or 1963 to the present), plus an arithmetic average of capital gain returns (over the same time horizons). To determine an estimate of shareholder taxes on each of these sources of income over the relevant historical period, we require the arithmetic average (from 1926 or 1963 to the present) for each of the following inputs:

- Effective federal and state income and capital gains tax rates (to calculate the amount of tax);
- Average holding period (to calculate the benefits of the deferral of capital gains tax); and
- Percentage of market held by tax-advantaged institutional investors (to calculate the extent that tax-advantaged institutional investment mitigates tax effects).

For each of the returns most commonly used by valuation analysts, these factors are presented in Exhibit 8-1.

Once these variables are known, calculating the taxes borne by public-market investors over the relevant time horizon is a fairly straightforward matter. The steps involve:

- A calculation of the dividend tax on income returns;
- A calculation of the capital gains tax, taking into consideration the deferral of such taxes over the holding period; and
- Considering the impact of tax-favored institutional investment by reducing the calculated taxes by the magnitude of tax-favored institutional investment.

As the data for different time horizons and returns differ, logically, the amount of penalty embedded in the market return will likewise vary.

95 For analysts not familiar with how Duff & Phelps calculates returns, please see Appendix C before reading further.

96 The tax penalty is not just the amount of taxes borne by public-market shareholders; it is further the extent to which such taxes actually affect value. Research has shown that, for the returns and time horizons studied, dividend and capital gains taxes do not directly affect value. While this latter factor serves to reduce the magnitude of the dividend tax penalty, this factor has not been examined for the historical returns used by analysts. Rather, we have suggested this as an area for further research (see Appendix A).

Exhibit 8-1. Arithmetic Average Returns and Variables Necessary to Calculate Embedded Taxes*

	Arithmetic Average					
Return Metric:	Income Return	Capital Gain Return	Effective Individual Income Tax Rate	Effective Capital Gains Tax Rate	Holding Period	Tax-Favored Institutional Investment
1963 to present, large stocks, WITH D&P recommended adjustment	3.3%	8.2%	21.2%	19.5%	2.7	26.2%
1926 to present, large stocks	4.1%	7.7%	20.6%	16.0%	3.8	16.5%
1926 to present, large stocks, supply side	4.1%	6.9%	20.6%	16.0%	3.8	16.5%
1926 to present, 10th decile	0.0%	21.2%	20.6%	16.0%	3.8	5.0%

* Notes:

- The source and calculations for the historical data provided in this chart are as follows; note that long-horizon (1963 to 2013 or 1926 to 2013) arithmetic averages were calculated for all data points:
- *Income returns, large stocks:* Ibbotson, *SBBI 2014 Classic Yearbook,* "Market Results for Stocks, Bonds, Bills and Inflation, 1926-2013," Morningstar, 2014 Table A-2 p. 198-199.
- *Total return, 10th decile:* Morningstar, *SBBI 2014 Classic Yearbook,* "Market Results for Stocks, Bonds, Bills and Inflation, 1926-2013," 2014, p. 103-104; calculated by taking the arithmetic average of the annual change in the NYSE/AMEX/NASDAQ Index Value for 10th decile as presented in the *SBBI 2014 Classic Yearbook*, Table 7-3 (pages 103-104), which is 21.2% since 1926; we compared this to the Duff & Phelps' *2014 Valuation Handbook—Guide to Cost of Capital*, Market Results Through 2013, page 4-3, which indicates that the total return on 10th decile stocks (1926-2013) is 20.85% (which agrees with our calculation of the total return for the 10th decile utilizing Table 7-2 of the *SBBI 2014 Classic Yearbook*). Notably, this leaves nothing for income return component..
- *Capital gain return, 10th decile:* Morningstar, *SBBI 2014 Classic Yearbook,* "Market Results for Stocks, Bonds, Bills and Inflation, 1926-2013," 2014, p. 103-104. Note that virtually the entire 10th decile arithmetic average return is comprised of capital gain returns.
- *Capital gain returns:* S&P 500 Index, available from FactSet, www.factset.com/.
- *Income tax rates:* "Table 1—All Individual Income Tax Returns: Sources of Income and Tax Items, Tax Years 1913-2005," www.taxpolicycenter.org/taxfacts/listdocs.cfm?topic3id=39andtopic2id=30 and estimated percent in the highest individual income tax bracket 1911-2012 www.taxpolicycenter.org/taxfacts/displayafact.cfm?Docid=543. In deriving the tax rate to apply to long horizon dividends, we have weighted the high and effective rates, utilizing data for the top 1% of income shares from 1926 to 2012.
- *Federal effective capital gains tax rates:* Tax Foundation, taxfoundation.org/article/federal-capital-gains-tax-collections-1954-2009.
- *State effective capital gains tax rates:* The National Bureau of Economic Research, "Top State Tax Rates." Source: www.nber.org/taxsim/state-rates. Last modified: April 2013. (Note that we have assumed that effective state tax rates are half the top rates. Data from 1977 to the present.)
- *Institutional investment:* The 2010 Institutional Investment Report, Trends in Institutional Investor Assets and Equity Ownership of U.S. Corporations, The Conference Board; note that not all years are reported; we inferred holding rates from the data that were available. Note further that 10th decile stocks are assumed to have only a very minor amount (5%) of tax-favored institutional investment, likely a conservative assumption.
- *Holding periods:* NYSE Factbook, "Turnover," www.nyxdata.com/Data-Products/Facts-and-Figures.

As an example of how the magnitude of taxes can be calculated, Exhibit 8-2 approximates the magnitude of the tax penalty embedded in the historical return for large capitalization stocks, measured from 1926 to the present.

The embedded dividend tax component is determined by multiplying the dividend return by the arithmetic average of the income tax rate. The embedded capital gain tax component is determined by multiplying the capital gain component by the arithmetic average of the capital gains tax rate. As public-market stockholders have the ability to defer these taxes, the capital gain component is present-valued at the arithmetic average holding period, using the total return as the discount rate.[97] Finally, the shareholder

97 The use of the total return is based on the assumption that, if the shareholder taxes were not due, the funds could have been reinvested back into the market, earning the total return.

Exhibit 8-2. Demonstration of Calculation of Embedded Tax in Historical Return								
Embedded Taxes, SUPPLY-SIDE Long-Horizon Large-Cap Stock Returns, 1926 to Present								
	Return	Effective Tax Rate, Fed. & State	Shareholder Tax	Holding Period	Present Value Rate	Present Value of Tax	Percent Tax-Favored Institutional	Embedded Tax Affect
Income return	4.1%	20.6%	0.8%			0.8%	16.5%	0.70%
Capital gain return	6.9%	16.0%	1.1%	3.77	11.0%	0.75%	16.5%	0.63%
Total embedded taxes								1.3%

taxes are multiplied by 1 minus the arithmetic average of the percentage of the market held by tax-favored institutional investors.

Critically: This calculation will produce a different adjustment depending on the period upon which the return used by the analyst is calculated (i.e., 1926 to the present, versus 1963 to the present, and large versus small capitalization stocks). This is because tax regimes have varied over time, resulting in different taxes (and tax penalties) being embedded in the returns. Similarly, large capitalization stocks have different embedded taxes than small capitalization stocks.

Removing the embedded dividend and capital gains taxes from the discount rate results in a cost of capital that is properly matched to the pass-through entity's cash flow (calculated after consideration of tax on corporate income). To calculate the discount rate without the impact of the embedded tax, the amount calculated as the embedded tax is removed (subtracted) from the discount rate.

For example, a 1.3% adjustment (as estimated in Exhibit 8 2) to a previously determined, unadjusted cap rate of 15% would imply an effective 9.5% "premium" for the value of a pass-through entity compared to public market investors, as shown in Exhibit 8-3.

Exhibit 8-3. Demonstration of Implied Premium (Large-Cap Stock Return)		
After-tax cash flow	$600	$600
Capitalization rate	15.0%	13.7%
Indicated value	$4,000	$4,380
"Premium"		**9.5%**

Note that even this may be overstated because subtracting the entire embedded tax assumes that taxes directly correlate with value. As discussed in Chapter 7, research has shown that this is not the case. Recall that Dhaliwal et al. found a relationship between the ex ante measures of cost of capital used in their analysis and the tax penalty of only

0.4 to 0.5.[98] This finding is further supported by our study of S versus C corporation commercial-bank transactions, discussed in Appendix D.

The indicated premium is less than the maximum premium derived from the S corp models, which generally find a premium in the range of 15% to a maximum of 25%. Given the fact that, over time, effective tax rates are lower than the statutory rate, and given strategies firms and investors employ to avoid or defer taxes, this finding makes sense. The extent of institutional investors in the market further affects the magnitude of embedded taxes.

The premium found by this method is also notably less than that calculated in Exhibit 6-5, which uses the same assumptions. This is important to note: The cash flow-based models ascribe the same magnitude of premium, *regardless of the cost of capital otherwise determined for the pass-through entity*. However, as the cost of capital increases, it necessarily indicates that there are increasingly other factors that weigh into the value of the company.

This is a concept analysts are familiar with from the application of a size premium. Consider, for example, the impact on value of a 5% addition to the cost of capital for size, applied to a company with a 15% versus a 20% cost of capital (before application of the size adjustment) as shown in Exhibit 8-4.

Exhibit 8-4. Effect of Size Adjustment on Cost of Capital		
Net cash flow	$1,000	$1,000
Capitalization rate before consideration of size	15%	20%
Indicated value, if no size premium	$6,667	$5,000
Size premium	5%	5%
Total capitalization rate	20%	25%
Indicated value	$5,000	$4,000
Reduction in value due to size	$1,667	$1,000
Percentage reduction in value due to size	**25%**	**20%**

Like the impact of size, *the impact of embedded taxes will have a varying effect, depending on the totality of the factors that affect the cost of capital*. The cash flow-based models fail to consider this, which could lead to an under- or overvaluation when they are employed.

Further, the impact of any tax adjustment is even more pronounced if a weighted average cost of capital (WACC) is used. The cash flow-based models ascribe the same

98 We have identified this as an area that warrants further research in Appendix A.

premium irrespective of the capital structure. However, the cost of debt is unaffected by the presence of shareholder taxes. In calculating the WACC, shareholder tax affects only the equity component of the capital structure.[99] This is demonstrated in Exhibit 8-5.

Exhibit 8-5. Demonstration of Tax Adjustment When WACC Is Employed

	WACC Weights	Public C Corp	S Corp
After-tax cash flow		$600	$600
Equity capitalization rate	60.0%	15.0%	13.7%
Debt rate	40.0%	3.0%	3.0%
WACC		10.2%	9.4%
Indicated value		$5,882	$6,369
"Premium"		**8.3%**	

In a 2002 study of S versus C corporation pricing, Dr. Terrance Jalbert found that "the method by which the firm is taxed affects the value of the firm as well as the capital structure the firm will adopt.... [Pass-through firms] have a higher value per dollar of [net operating income] than [double-taxed firms].... *The differential in value is mitigated among firms that use higher levels of debt.*" (emphasis added)[100,101] A summary of Dr. Jalbert's study is found in Appendix D.

Summary. Academic research demonstrates that the tax penalty manifests itself in reduced prices investors are willing to pay for public-market stocks, having the effect of increasing public-market returns. Private-market valuation analysts use these public-market returns to value private companies whose investors don't experience dividend and capital gains taxes and, as such, the value of the private company should not reflect the effects of the shareholder tax penalty. Accordingly, this guide suggests that valuation analysts consider making an adjustment to the market return to remove the effect of the shareholder tax penalty from it, much in the same way that analysts adjust for size, liquidity, and other factors. In the alternative, analysts could adjust the cost of capital in the manner presented in Exhibit 5-1. In either case, the critical issue

99 The cost of debt is impacted by debt-holder taxes (not shareholder taxes) just as our bond example demonstrates. The equilibrium capital structure changes as any of three taxes (shareholder, debt-holder and corporate taxes) change.

100 "Pass-Through Taxation and the Value of the Firm" by Dr. Terrance Jalbert, assistant professor of finance, University of Hawaii, published in *American Business Review*, June, 2002, page 5.

101 The author's review of *Pratt's Stats* data confirms that pass-through firms have a higher operating income than double-taxed firms. This is likely because double-taxed firms (most notably, those under $50 million in revenue) are generally incentivized to reduce bottom-line profits (thereby mitigating the effects of double taxation).

is to properly match the cash flows being valued with the cost of capital employed in the valuation model.

Importantly, the research demonstrates that company-specific and shareholder-specific attributes play a significant part in determining the magnitude, if any, of the impact of shareholder-level taxes on the cost of equity of public companies. Not only do these attributes vary across firms, but they also have varied significantly over time and, most critically, are frequently unobservable. Moreover, several of these company-specific and shareholder-specific attributes *interact*, and that interaction takes place in a market where companies are free to adjust their payout strategies and investors are free to constantly re-evaluate and reposition their investment decisions based on current, actual, and anticipated changes in their individual tax situation, overall tax regimes, cash-flow needs, and changes in corporate dividend policy.

Any calculated estimate of the impact of the mismatch between the public-market return and a pass-through entity is only that: an estimate. However, it rests on the academic research discussed in this guide. To date, the inputs to the S corp models, the Delaware Chancery model, and the no tax affect model all rest largely on unsupported hypotheses. At the very least, the research presented herein allows the analyst to make informed choices about the inputs to these models.

Appendix A. Suggested Areas for Further Research

We noted in the Introduction that this guide has been seven years in the making. As one of our technical reviewers, a researcher himself, said to us, "You'll never be done." Research is meant to be continually furthered and improved upon, and this work is no exception. At the time of this writing, we note the following key areas upon which we hope to expand this research in the future.

Areas where further research is warranted include the following:

1. Although we can make a calculation of the estimated amount of tax paid by public-market investors, Dhaliwal et al. found that a regression analysis demonstrated a relationship between the ex ante measures of cost of capital used in their analysis and the tax penalty of approximately 0.4 to 0.5. This indicates that, just because public-market investors paid personal (dividend and capital gains) taxes, the taxes paid do not directly correlate with value. The cash flow-based models all assume that they do, by utilizing 100% of the current statutory tax rate. Additional research can and should be done to test the extent to which the presence of personal taxes actually had an impact on the value of the public-market firms.

2. The cash flow-based models primarily seek to account for the avoidance of dividend and capital gains taxes by pass-through entities, compared to that which is embedded in the public-market returns. However, the cash flow-based models also require consideration of the magnitude of effective taxes borne by public C corporations over time. Further research on the amount and effect of these taxes is warranted, especially their impact on corporate cost of equity capital.

3. Additional research might also be made into the extent to which the level of debt affects this discussion. In general, studies have found (and *Pratt's Stats* data confirm) that C corporations generally have higher levels of debt in their capital structure than pass-through entities. The access of C corporations to cheaper capital likely affects the prices C corporation buyers are willing to pay; indeed, public C corporation buyers typically pay as much as twice what private buyers (often S corporations or individuals) pay for similar companies (confirmed by our bank study discussed in Appendix D). At the same time, the lower levels of debt capital accessed by S corporations may hinder their value. These factors may serve to influence this discussion, as more becomes known.

4. The benefits of a 338(h)(10) election has gotten little attention in private-valuation circles. More consideration of this potentially valuable election is warranted.

5. Several studies comparing transaction pricing multiples between S corporations and C corporations have found little or no difference in pricing. These studies are discussed in Appendix D. In fact, if anything, they find C corporation pricing to be greater than S corporation pricing. A notable exception to this is the research done by Dr. Erickson (see Appendix D), which finds a premium related to a 338(h)(10) election. The authors' study on a large number of commercial bank sales, which controls for any 338 effects, finds no premium for sub S corporations. Further work can be done to examine and refine these findings.

6. To the extent that private C corporations (particularly small ones, those under $50 million in revenue) mimic the benefits of pass-through entities, they, too, may have a tax differential relative to the public market return.

7. On the basis of the research available to us, we have assumed only a nominal level of tax-exempt institutional investment in small-stock returns. More research can be done to determine a more accurate estimate of these stock holdings.

8. High frequency trading has had a significant effect on holding periods. The data presented herein are based on turnover of the New York Stock Exchange, which demonstrates that holding periods have declined dramatically in recent decades. In addition, some research demonstrates that a significant share of U.S. stocks held by individuals was being held until death to avoid the large capital gains that had accrued. Further research is warranted on the effects of both of these issues on market pricing and holding period.

9. The taxes borne on dividends are more difficult to estimate than are taxes on capital gains. This is because capital gains, and the taxes on them, are separately reported on individual income tax returns, whereas dividends are included in total taxable income (and, therefore, total tax). More research needs to be done on the magnitude and effect of dividend taxes.

We welcome input and thoughtful comments related to this guide, as well as the areas in which additional research would be helpful to our analysis. We also welcome additional research that is relevant to the issues discussed herein.

Appendix B. Evolution of Pass-Through Entity Valuation

Pass-through entity valuation has perplexed valuation analysts for years. As far back as the early 1990s, analysts were questioning whether or how the value of S corporations and other pass-through entities should be adjusted for tax issues. Unfortunately, before the private-company valuation community had reached any coherent solution to the issue (or had even figured out what it was adjusting for), the U.S. Tax Court weighed in with its decision in the now-infamous *Gross* case in 1999.

Seven memorandum decisions by the U.S. Tax Courts have addressed the question of how taxes affect value in a pass-through entity. In each case, the Tax Court disallowed (or endorsed the disallowance of) a deduction for taxes of any sort on corporate income because it was the shareholders, and not the corporation, who were responsible for those taxes.

These cases are:

- *Gross v. Commissioner,* T.C. Memo. 1999-254, aff'd, 272 F.3d 333 F.3d (6th Cir. 2001);
- *Wall v. Commissioner,* T.C. Memo. 2001-75;
- *Adams v. Commissioner,* T.C. Memo. 2002-80;
- *Heck v. Commissioner,* T.C. Memo. 2002-34;
- *Dallas v. Commissioner,* T.C. Memo. 2006-21;
- *Estate of Gallagher v. Commissioner,* T.C. Memo 2011-148; and
- *Estate of Giustina v. Commissioner,* 2014 U.S. App. LEXIS 22961 (Dec. 5, 2014).

Abstracts of each of these court cases can be found in Appendix E.

The Tax Court first broached the issue of a potential valuation differential for entities taxed under different regimes in 1999 in *Gross v. Commissioner*.[102] In an otherwise unremarkable case (which was eventually appealed to the Supreme Court but denied a hearing), expert witnesses for the IRS and the taxpayers utilized very similar income approaches for estimating the fair market value of a closely held company. However, their similar models yielded substantially different values. This difference in value was primarily due to the fact that the taxpayer's expert reduced the projected future stream of income from the company by what the Tax Court labeled a "fictitious" tax burden, a process that he referred to as "tax affecting":

> [Taxpayer's expert] further testified that, in order to comply with the (professional) standards rule, it was necessary for professional appraisers to "tax affect" the earnings of an S Corporation in order to produce a credible business appraisal. To accomplish such tax affecting, [taxpayer's expert] assumed a corporate tax rate of 40%, which he applied to reduce each future period's earnings, before such earnings were discounted to their present value.

The IRS's expert estimated fair market value using the present value of a similarly forecasted stream of earnings. However, no corporate-level taxes were imputed in his calculations. Given this construction, the IRS's expert's model would yield a fair market value 67% higher than the taxpayer's expert, all other variables being equal.[103]

In support of tax affecting the earnings, the taxpayer's expert introduced language from two IRS documents: *A Valuation Guide for Income Estate* and *Gift Taxes* and *Examination Technique Guide for Estate Tax Examiners*. Quoting the IRS valuation guide, the taxpayer's expert asserted that the IRS guidance explicitly accepted the need to "tax affect" the earnings of pass-through entities:

102 The only prior case using the term "tax affecting" was a non-tax-related case tried in the Delaware Chancery Court. See *Radiology Associates, Inc.*, 611 A.2d 485, 495 (Del. Ch. 1991).

103 In its discussion, the court noted that "the decision whether to tax affect G&J's projected earnings under the discounted cash-flow approach accounts for the most significant differences between the parties' expert witnesses." In fact, after adjusting for this one factor, the IRS's expert's value was less than 10% higher than the taxpayer's expert's. The IRS purportedly selected this valuation to litigate because it had facts it considered favorable to its argument, specifically, that the company had constant growth in income and distributions, and distributions were on the order of 99% of income. However, the issue of the magnitude of distributions is a red herring; if the funds are not distributed, then they benefit the shareholders through a growth in the value of the company. As this text discusses, the real question is whether the cost of capital matches the income stream.

> S Corporations are treated similarly to partnerships for tax purposes. S Corporations lend themselves readily to valuation approaches comparable to those used in valuing closely held corporations. You need only to adjust the earnings from the business to reflect estimated corporate income taxes that would have been payable had the Subchapter S election not been made.

Similarly, a quote from the IRS guide asserted:

> If you are comparing a Subchapter S Corporation to the stock of similar firms that are publicly traded, the net income of the former must be adjusted for income taxes using the corporate tax rates applicable for each year in question, and certain other items, such as salaries. These adjustments will avoid distortions when applying industry ratios such as price to earnings.

Based on these excerpts, it could be argued that the IRS materials accepted, and even required, the imputation of entity-level taxes when estimating fair market value of subchapter S corporations. However, the Tax Court rejected this conclusion, asserting that the excerpts "lack analytical support" and, in any event, did not "have the force of a regulation or ruling."[104]

In a final attempt to sway the court, the taxpayer hired a second expert, an appraiser and valuation expert, to prepare a report in rebuttal of the IRS expert's testimony. In his testimony, the taxpayer's second expert made perhaps the most sound and compelling argument at that time in favor of tax affecting:

> In effect, an S Corporation is committed to making distributions to shareholders sufficient to cover individual tax liabilities on allocated S Corporation earnings in the same fashion that a C Corporation is committed to making tax payments to the Service to cover corporate tax liabilities on reported taxable earnings. Whether the outflow is a cash distribution made by an S Corporation to satisfy shareholders' tax liabilities, or the direct payment of a tax liability by a C Corporation, the decrease in cash experienced by either entity represents a known payment which reduces the availability of cash which could otherwise be used to maintain or expand existing operations. Such a decrease must be taken into consideration when valuing an entity, whether it is structured as a C Corporation or an S Corporation.

104 At appeal, the court noted that both IRS guides explicitly state that they are "not to be relied upon as binding authority."

Unfortunately, the taxpayer's second expert failed to produce analytical evidence or examples to convincingly demonstrate, much less quantify, the decrease in value resulting from any required distributions or subsequent shareholder-level taxes.[105] If the expert had been able to produce the research on the impact of shareholder-level taxes on value discussed throughout this guide, the taxpayer may well have prevailed in the *Gross* case, which could have resulted in a profoundly different effect on valuation since that time.

Lacking such evidence, the court was unwilling to reduce the earnings stream for taxes on income, concluding that "the principal benefit that shareholders expect from an S Corporation election is a reduction in the *total tax burden imposed on the enterprise*. The owners expect to save money, and we see no reason why that savings ought to be ignored as a matter of course in valuing the S Corporation." (emphasis added)

The language the court used in this instance is a bit surprising, given the fact that neither the experts nor the court attempted any analysis of "total tax burden" imposed on enterprise earnings. As we will discuss throughout this guide, it is the effect of the "total tax burden" that leads to a differential in value between a public C corporation and an S corporation. A 2013 report prepared for the SBA Office of Advocacy agrees with this position, stating:

> While official tax expenditure estimates provide a breakdown between the individual income tax and the corporate income tax, this breakdown is inadequate for an analysis that proposes to examine the impact of tax expenditures on all small businesses. Because many small businesses (i.e., sole proprietorships, partnerships, and S corporations) are not subject to the corporate income tax, any analysis that attempts to measure the effects of tax expenditures on all small businesses *must take into account the business tax effects incorporated in the individual income tax expenditure estimates.*[106] (emphasis added)

Notwithstanding this, *Gross v. Commissioner* established a precedent[107] (at least for cases with similar fact patterns as the *Gross* case) of ignoring all shareholder-level taxes, an approach that artificially increases the appraised fair market value of virtually any

105 We can't help but wonder whether the Tax Court might have made a different determination if evidence had been produced that demonstrated the company was legally required to pay taxes to their shareholder quarterly (such as is found in many S corporation shareholder agreements), had a history proving that they did so, and that the shareholders then paid the tax.

106 John O'Hare, Mary Schmitt, Judy Xanthopoulos, "Measuring the Benefit of Federal Tax Expenditures Used by Small Business," Quantria Strategies LLC, prepared for use by the SBA Office of Advocacy, page 34.

107 However such precedence is nonbinding, as the decision—and all those that followed it—are memorandum decisions only.

pass-through entity, compared to a publicly traded C corporation (the source of the return used to value the pass-through entity). The taxpayers in the *Gross* case appealed the case, but the Court of Appeals affirmed the determination. In its discussion, the Court of Appeals for the 6th Circuit[108] noted primarily that the taxpayers carried the burden of proof and they failed to prove that the Tax Court had erred in its approach.

> Indeed, *taxpayers have yet to provide the burden of proof required to demonstrate the fact and manner in which shareholder taxes affect value*. Accordingly, since the *Gross* case, the Tax Court has consistently rejected the concept of tax affecting in subsequent cases involving the valuation of Subchapter S Corporations.[109] (emphasis added)

To our knowledge, as of this writing, this proof has yet to be presented to the Tax Court.

As noted earlier, several private-company valuation professionals reacted to the decisions of the U.S. Tax Court by designing models that recognized that, while pass-through entity investors do not avoid taxes on corporate income, compared to their publicly traded counterparts, they do avoid dividend and capital gains taxes. The S corporation models, created by Chris Treharne, Daniel Van Vleet, Roger Grabowski, and Christopher Mercer (the S corp models), all appeared to be very different. However, at their core, they all did the same thing: recognized the benefit of avoiding dividend and capital gains tax, compared with public-market investors.

A 2006 decision by the Delaware Chancery Court[110] recognized the work that the valuation profession had done in creating the S corp models and agreed that the benefit of pass-through entity status was in the avoidance of dividend and capital gains taxes and not in any avoidance of taxes on corporate income.[111] In that case, the court derived its own model to account for the avoidance of dividend and capital gains taxes by S

108 All other circuits have been silent on this issue.

109 Subsequent Tax Court Cases include *Wall v. Commissioner*, T.C. Memo 2001-75, *Adams v. Commissioner*, T.C. Memo 2002-80, *Heck v. Commissioner*, T.C. Memo 2002-34, *Dallas v. Commissioner*, T.C. Memo 2006-212, and *Gallagher v. Commissioner*, T.C. Memo 2011-148. In each case, the court specifically considered and rejected tax affecting. In no case did the court provide a description of what set of facts and circumstances would warrant tax affecting, nor has the Tax Court accepted any alternative methodology for differentiating the value of pass-through and non-pass-through entities.

110 *Delaware Open MRI Radiology Associates, P.A. v. Kessler*, CA-275-N, 2006 Del. Ch. LEXIS 84 (2006).

111 The *Dallas* case made a distinction between value as determined by the Tax Court (fair market value) and by the Delaware Chancery (fair value), indicating the differences in the standard of value employed were the reason for the Tax Court to reject what the Delaware Chancery had done. The IRS has frequently repeated this reasoning. However, as this guide discussed, the adjustment made by analysts is to remove an effect that is embedded in the public-market return used in the application of the income approach. However, there is no difference in the derivation of the return an analyst uses for a fair market value versus a fair value determination, which, as this guide discusses, is the crux of the issue.

corporation investors (commonly referred to as the Delaware Chancery model). The position of the Delaware Chancery Court was later adopted in a case before the Supreme Judicial Court of Massachusetts.[112] These cases are also included in Appendix E.

112 *Judith E. Bernier v. Stephen A. Bernier*, (82 Mass. App. Ct. 81). Note that some have interpreted the result of the long-suffering *Bernier* case (first heard in 2002 but not ultimately decided until 2012) as a denial of any deduction for taxes. This belief is because, in employing the Delaware Chancery model, the Supreme Judicial Court of Massachusetts applied a strict interpretation and determined that the appropriate dividend tax rate to use in the model was 40%—the rate that was in effect at the valuation date. Doing so resulted in the same *math exercise* as if the Supreme Judicial Court had disallowed any deduction for taxes (a result the court itself noted). Following the court's findings, a valuation analyst today would employ the current, lower dividend tax rate. However, as has been discussed throughout this guide, even this is misguided and would overstate the impact of embedded taxes (as it significantly did in the ultimate Supreme Judicial Court decision). Unfortunately, no expert provided the court any evidence upon which it could have based such a determination. Further, if a similarly strict interpretation of corporate tax rates were employed in the Delaware Chancery model, the model would indicate a *detriment* for the S corporation.

Appendix C. Understanding the Basics of the Cost of Capital

When applying the income approach to valuing both private and public companies, analysts typically rely on historical returns derived from the public stock market as the foundation for calculating the equity risk premium (ERP) and the cost of capital. By using market-derived returns, analysts implicitly assume that the risks of the subject company are quantitatively similar to the risks of the average company in the subject portfolio.[113]

To the extent that the subject company differs from the "average company in the portfolio" underlying the equity risk premium, the analyst considers adjustments to the cost of capital. This is precisely what analysts do when they make adjustments to the cost of capital for size, illiquidity, or specific company risks. That is, because the subject company differs from the public market used to value it, the public-market return is adjusted to compensate for those differences.

It is no different with the issue of shareholder taxes. Shareholder-level taxes that are embedded in market returns likely differ from the taxes imposed on the particular public or private company that the analyst is valuing. Accordingly, the analyst should consider an adjustment to the market-derived return. Analysts frequently adjust cost of capital estimates for identifiable, company-specific factors. Tax attributes should be added to the list of factors to consider.

113 See generally Shannon P. Pratt and Roger J. Grabowski, *Cost of Capital: Applications and Examples* (3rd ed. Wiley, 2008) (hereinafter *Cost of Capital*, 2008).

Why start with the cost of capital? The cost of capital has generally been defined as "the before-tax required return on an asset."[114] The term "before tax" means that the market returns analysts use to value public and private companies is before investor-level taxes.[115] Thus, when analysts use a cost of capital derived from publicly traded companies, they should adjust it for differences in shareholder-level taxes (unless it is proper to assume that shareholder-level taxes are the same for the publicly traded companies and the company they are valuing, as one might assume for a private C corporation).

The returns that analysts obtain from the public markets are after taxes on corporate income. Value, which has the fundamental elements of: (1) the cost of capital; (2) expected growth; and (3) income, is similarly calculated after taxes on corporate income. This is self-evident when you consider that the value of any financial asset, including most "real" or fixed assets (such as industrial plants) depends on the stream of cash flows that the asset produces—that is, an asset's *usable* income. Usable income means income after (corporate) taxes.[116] The same theory holds true for entire enterprises.[117]

However, a distinction between the return and the income stream to which it is applied arises with respect to the impact of shareholder taxes on value. Public-market returns include the negative effects of shareholder taxes on value. As S corporation investors do not bear such taxes, these effects should be removed.

To properly make an adjustment to remove or adjust the amount of tax (or other adjustments, such as size and liquidity) embedded in the market return, it is first necessary to understand the derivation of the market return—in other words, an adjustment can't be made *to* something without first understanding how the thing being adjusted *for* affects it.

The issue of whether and how much shareholder taxes affect value and the cost of capital has been the subject of extensive academic research that spans many years and various theories. All such research is grounded in the fundamental elements of market

114 Sinn, 1991.

115 Dan Dhaliwal, Linda Krull, Oliver Zhen Li, and William Moser, "Dividend Taxes and the Implied Cost of Equity Capital," *Journal of Accounting Research*, December 2005, Vol. 43, No. 5, p. 684.

116 Eugene F. Brigham and Joel F. Houston, *Fundamentals of Financial Management*, Thomson South-Western, Division of Thomson Learning, 1998, p. 47.

117 For example, usable income for a corporate entity is that which is available after corporate income taxes are paid, whether the corporation pays them directly or passes them through to the shareholders. Either way, the income is not "useable" by the corporation to fund growth and value. The distinction between these two discrete types of a tax—that is, a tax on income and shareholder tax—is critically important to understanding how public-market returns are derived, what they represent, and how analysts use them in valuation.

returns;[118] without this foundation, it is impossible to have a meaningful dialogue on the effect of shareholder tax on value.

Thus, this appendix provides an overview of public-market returns, a critical element of the cost of capital. Once analysts understand the shareholder taxes embedded in market returns, they can evaluate the subject company to determine whether an adjustment should be made to account for any tax differential.

Sources of data. Duff & Phelps provides an annual update of historical return data. Data are provided for income and capital gain returns, measuring periods either from 1926 to present or from 1963 to the present.

There are numerous other ways to develop a market return in addition to obtaining one from a commercial source, each of which has an inherent tax component. The focus of this guide is the commercially available data that analysts most commonly use: long horizon returns provided by Duff & Phelps. We encourage the reader to review the materials that accompany this data source thoroughly to fully understand its proper application.

Components of market returns. The most significant components of the annually reported market return combines dividend and capital gains components. When shareholders receive a dividend or incur capital gains by virtue of selling their shares, they may incur a dividend or realize a capital gains tax. It is these personal taxes, dividend and capital gains taxes, that the academic literature has studied extensively and demonstrated the effect on corporate value.[119]

For example, a 2005 study by Dhaliwal, Krull, Li, and Moser finds:

> If [public] stock prices capitalize [dividend and capital gains] taxes, the discount rate implied by the relation between these values will reflect investor-level taxes on

118 "Market returns" as used in this text generally refers to the total returns obtained from the public stock market, including returns on income and capital gains taxes. This term is used at times interchangeably with "total returns," as this section describes. This guide provides only a general background of market returns necessary for understanding the effect of shareholder taxes on value; we encourage the reader to familiarize themselves with a more complete analysis found in *Valuation Handbook - Guide to Cost of Capital*, Duff & Phelps, and Ibbotson *SBBI Classic Yearbook, Market Results for Stocks, Bonds, Bills, and Inflation*, Morningstar, each updated annually.

119 This is not to suggest that investors do not value strategies by which corporate managers seek to minimize or avoid income taxes; however, all corporate forms, both public and private, pay taxes on corporate income, and the federal and state government collects income taxes on all corporate profits, whether public or private—the distinction being, in some forms of private ownership, the taxes on corporate profits "pass through" to the owners. To the investor, this makes no difference, as the firm cannot use that money to fuel growth and value. As noted in Appendix A, the impact of corporate income taxes is an area where further research is warranted.

> the expected dividend stream ... the implied cost of equity capital, *r e*, will reflect investor-level taxes on equity, that is, *r e* is the before-tax required return.[120]

Why do shareholder dividend and capital gain taxes have an effect on value? Simply put, investors seek to avoid taxes and corporate firms need investors to invest in those firms. As a result, investors change investment strategies to take advantage of tax strategies, firms change payout strategies to attract and accommodate investors,[121] and both investors and firms take advantage of the applicable tax laws. Thus, while shareholder-level taxes impact value, these combined actions effectively reduce the overall impact of shareholder taxes on value.

As a result, we break down calculation of the equity risk premium and the market return into its component parts—income, capital gains, and bond returns—so that we can examine the effect that taxes have on shareholders and, consequently, the market return and value.

Derivation of the cost of capital for the income approach. As a general overview, market returns are typically calculated in the context of the capital asset pricing model (CAPM) as set forth in Exhibit C-1.

Exhibit C-1. Calculation of Market Returns	
	Arithmetic average of income portion of market return (dividend returns)
+	Arithmetic average of capital gain returns (changes in the value of the stock market/index)*
+	Reinvestment returns (return on investment income when reinvested into the same asset class in the subsequent months of the year
=	**Total market return**
-	Riskless rate (typically represented by the arithmetic average of the income portion of long-term government bond returns)
=	**Equity risk premium**
+	Current long-term government bond yield
=	**Total market return**

* Generally measured by the S&P 500, NYSE, or NYSE/AMEX/NASDAQ, as adjusted by the data provider.

The *dividend portion* of the market return is paid out of corporate net profits—that is, after the corporation has paid taxes on corporate income and has retained the capital necessary to fund growth and value.

120 Dan Dhaliwal, Linda Krull, Oliver Zhen Li, and William Moser, December 2005, "Dividend Taxes and the Implied Cost of Equity Capital," *Journal of Accounting Research*, Vol. 43, No. 5, p. 683-684.

121 Raj Chetty and Emmanuel Saez, "Dividend Taxes and Corporate Behavior: Evidence from the 2003 Dividend Tax Cut," *NBER Working Paper No. 10841*, Sept. 27, 2004.

- The *capital gains portion* of the market return is based on the growth in the value of the stock market from year-to-year (according to the change in the value of the particular stock market proxy that the data provider uses); and
- The *reinvestment return* is the return on investment income when reinvested into the same asset class in the subsequent months of the year.

Investors receive these corporate dividends based on the firm's payout policy, and they sell their shares in part based on the firm's payout strategy (for example, the firm might offer a buyback of shares), or the investor may decide to sell the shares in the marketplace. From these collective decisions, researchers can calculate average holding periods for various times in the market. Researchers have observed market returns and their composition over extended time horizons, during which many aspects were driven by payout policies, market participants, and, important for this discussion, tax policy.[122]

Duff & Phelps' reported market return is an average of all of the returns (dividend plus capital gain) from the period the respective sources began calculating returns to the present; most analysts of private businesses use arithmetic averages.[123]

Duff & Phelps calculates its returns as the long-horizon average from either 1929 to the present (familiar to many analysts as the former Ibbotson/Morningstar data) or 1963 to the present, relying on the Center for Research in Security Pricing (CRSP) database.

Using the S&P 500 as a proxy and the long-term realized total return for the 88-year period 1926 to 2013,[124] we can see in Exhibit C-2 that the income portion of the market return of large capitalization stocks has gone down in more recent years.

The capital gains portion of the total long-term historical return is made up of changes in the value of the stock market. When the long-term realized return is measured by changes in the S&P 500, the increase in the market value has been substantial in the more recent years.

122 See, for example, William Moser and Andy Puckett, "Dividend Tax Clienteles: Evidence From Tax Law Changes," 2008, p. 4, *Journal of the American Taxation Association* (JATA), Spring 2009, Volume 30, No. 1, aaajournals.org/doi/abs/10.2308/jata.2009.31.1.1.

123 Arithmetic averages are calculated by summing a set of numbers and dividing by total count (n) of numbers in the set. Duff & Phelps recommends the use of "smoothed" average historical risk premium; a smoothed average is the fitted premium from a regression with the average historical risk premium as dependent variable and the logarithm of the average sorting criteria as independent variable.

124 Data provided in this appendix were generally calculated using data provided by Morningstar (formerly Ibbotson Associates' "Ibbotson SBBI Valuation Yearbook Market Results for Stocks, Bonds, Bills and Inflation," beginning with 1926 data and updated annually). For 2013, it was supplemented by data from *Ibbotson SBBI 2014 Classic Yearbook, Market Results for Stocks, Bonds, Bills, and Inflation*, 1926-2013, and the *2014 Valuation Handbook - Guide to Cost of Capital*, Market Results Through 2013, Duff & Phelps.

Exhibits C-2 and C-3 demonstrate that the year-to-year changes in dividends and capital gains have been volatile. However, in the calculation of the arithmetic averages, the effect has been that the total realized return has become comprised more of capital gains than income returns, as seen in Exhibit C-4.

The volatility of average capital gain returns, as shown in Exhibit C-4, lessens over time as more years of data are added to the average. This demonstrates the importance of having an adequate period of time to calculate "average" historical returns.

Exhibit C-2. Income Portion of Total Market Return, Large-Cap Stocks, S&P 500, 1926-2013

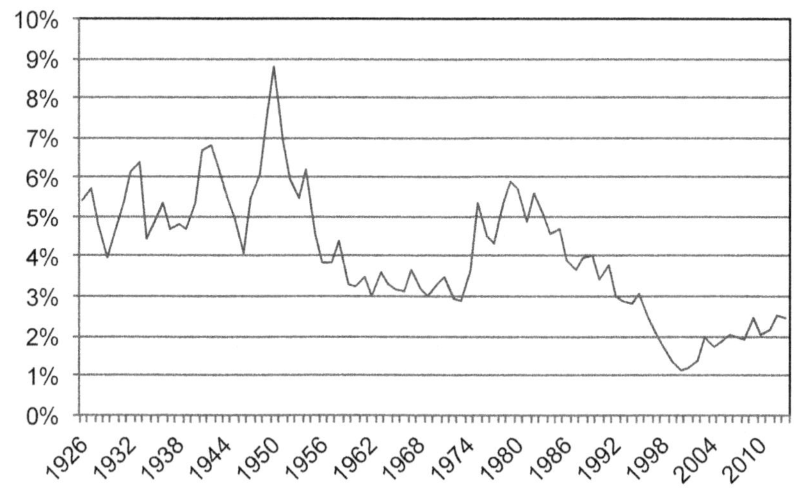

Exhibit C-3. S&P 500 Index, 1926-2013

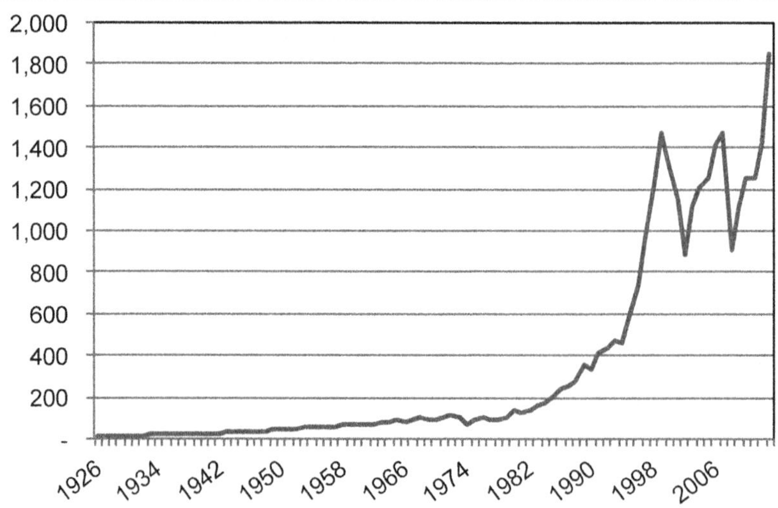

To derive the equity risk premium, the arithmetic average of the long-term government bond income returns is subtracted from the total return. These returns, shown in Exhibit C-5 on a "raw" basis (that is, not the arithmetic average), have been variable over the last 88 years.

The increase in the long-term bond yields, and our "riskless rate," began in the early 1960s, reached its peak in the 1980s, and has since come back down.

Exhibit C-4. Arithmetic Average Income and Capital Gain Portion of Total Market Return, Large Capitalization Stocks, S&P 500, 1926-2013

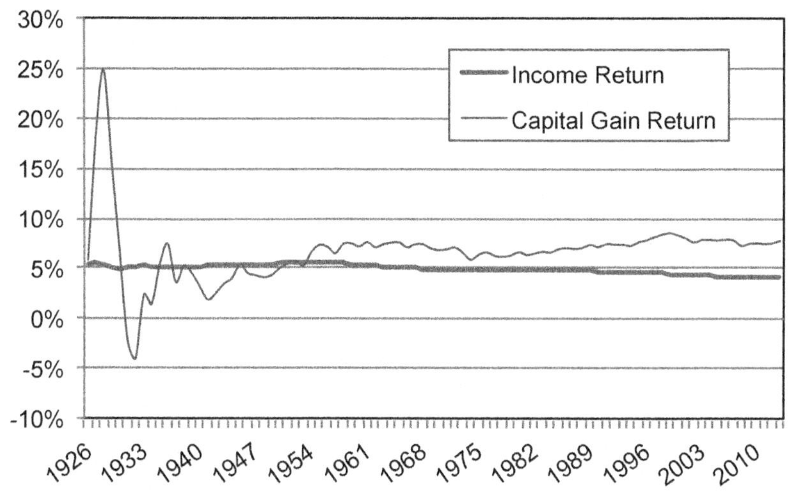

Exhibit C-5. Long-Term Government Bond Income Returns, 1926-2013

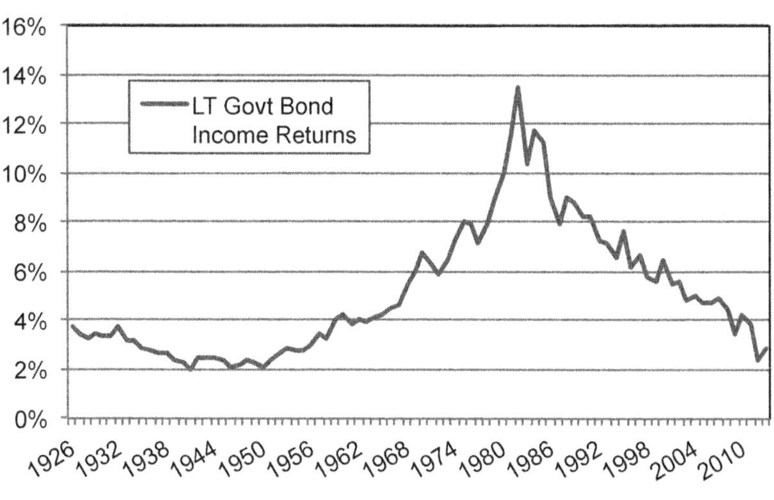

These three components have provided researchers decades of material to study and analyze regarding the causes of the movement of the stock market. As a result, market returns can be calculated in many ways, each of which requires certain assumptions to be made and each with its supporters and detractors.

When analysts use an arithmetic average market return, they are adopting the collective effect of all the influences that are "baked into" the average market return, over whatever period it has been calculated. Quoting Duff & Phelps' 2013 *Risk Premium Report:*

> Use of a portfolio's average historical rate of return to estimate a discount rate for a subject company is also based upon the implicit assumption that the risks of the subject company are quantitatively similar to the risks of the average company in the portfolio. If the risks of the subject company differ materially from the average company in the portfolio, then the estimated discount rate may be less than (or greater than) the discount rate derived using the risk premium or size premium associated with the given portfolio[125] ..., the risks of the subject company more than likely differ in some respects from the risks of the sample of guideline public companies it is being compared to.[126]

As of 2013, the market return that analysts use is an arithmetic average of 88 years when using Morningstar data or 51 years when using Duff & Phelps. The year 2013 is weighed no more heavily than the year 1929, 1963, 2009, or any other year. Thus, the "average company in the subject portfolio" is a blending of all of the implicit assumptions contained in the arithmetic average of the market return. To the extent that the subject company has a different profile—in terms of size, the effect of shareholder taxes, liquidity, or any other factors—then the analyst will need to adjust either the required rate of return, or the income stream, to make the calculation comparable.

Most analysts make their adjustment for shareholder taxes by tacking a "premium" onto the value of an S corporation or other pass-through entity for perceived differences between it and the public proxies we have used to estimate cost of capital. The premium is typically calculated by use of one of the S corp models or the Delaware Chancery model, previously discussed. Recognize, though, that this premium is just another way of expressing what is otherwise an adjustment to the market return—and this guide suggests analysts consider whether it should alternatively be treated as an adjustment to the market return, where it arises in the first place. However, that does not mean that the S corp models cannot continue to provide a good estimate of the

125 Duff & Phelps, 2013, p. 112.
126 Ibid., p. 113.

valuation differential, as long as the factors that dampen the tax effect in public-market returns are considered.

Time horizons. A compelling case can be made for using either a long-term historical risk premium (1926-present) or a shorter-term risk premium (1963-present). Using S&P data as a proxy, through 2013, the longer horizon total market return was 11.8%; by comparison, using 1963 to 2013, still using the S&P 500 as a proxy, the total market return was 11.6%.

An analyst who adopts either period inherently assumes that the inclusion of past events is a good predictor of the future. To occur in the past, these market returns—their causes and the values they represent—include the complex effects of shareholder taxes. In turn, these embedded tax effects vary depending on the underlying components of the market return.

The long-horizon total market return, calculated annually, effectively "smoothes out" these events. Exhibit C-6 demonstrates the total market return over both the two time horizons.

Exhibit C-6. Arithmetic Average Total Market Returns, 1926-2013, 1963-2013, S&P 500 Data

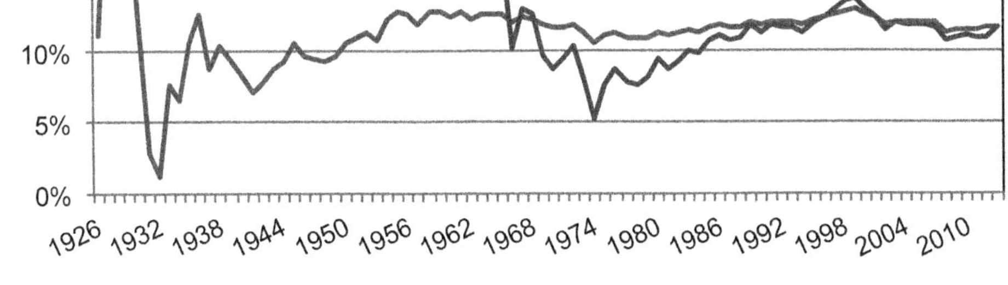

As one might expect, both measures stabilize over time and the total realized market returns for the two measures merge.

However, most analysts use the return in the context of CAPM, which requires the calculation of the ERP by subtracting the arithmetic average long-term government

Exhibit C-7. Arithmetic Average Long-Term Government Bond Income Returns, 1926-2013, 1963-2013, S&P 500 Data

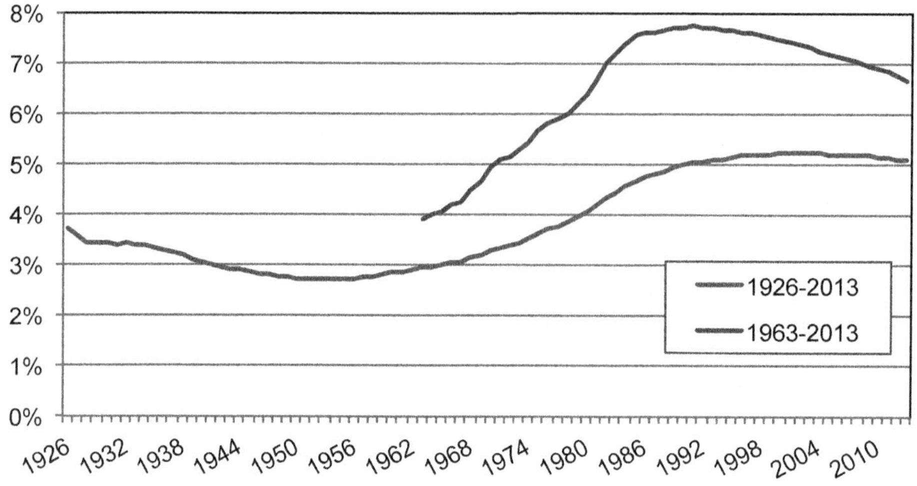

bond income returns from total market returns, as shown in Exhibit C-7 for the two time horizons.

Bond returns were much higher over the 1963-to-2013 period than over the longer term, but more recently they have returned to levels not seen since the mid-1970s. (For example, from 1926 through the mid-1980s, the arithmetic average long-term government bond income return was approximately 4.5%. The long-term government bond yield as of 2013 was 2.9%.) For the calculation of the 2013 ERP, for example, for the period 1926 to 2013, the long-horizon, long-term government bond income return is 5.1%. By comparison, for the period 1963 to 2013, the long-horizon government bond income return of 6.68%.[127]

There are many other ways of estimating the cost of capital to use in a valuation that are beyond the scope of this guide. The point of this discussion is to demonstrate the composition of the market returns that analysts most commonly use. Over time, as the composition of the market return has changed, the underlying effects that analysts must deal with have also changed. These underlying effects include liquidity, size, and tax effects. Relevant to this discussion is the assumption that the investor who receives the underlying component of the public-market return—dividends and capital gains—is taxed upon their receipt.

127 The effect of the Duff & Phelps recommended adjustment to the ERP and to the current bond return effectively removes the differential between these two time horizons.

Appendix D. C Corporation Versus S Corporation Transaction Pricing

Numerous studies have been done over the years comparing purchase prices of S corporations and C corporations. These studies have alternately found either no premium in S corporation pricing or that C corporation pricing is higher. They also bring to light areas where additional research would be helpful.

A summary of these studies follows.

"Pass-Through Taxation and the Value of the Firm" by Dr. Terrance Jalbert, assistant professor of finance, University of Hawaii, published in *American Business Review*, June, 2002

Dr. Jalbert began with an examination of prior research, including work by Jeffrey Jaffe who, in 1991, conducted a study on the impact of capital structure and taxes on pass-through entities, as well as David Guenther's 1992 study comparing pass-through entities and double-taxed entities. Guenther found that, while double-taxed firms have higher tax costs, pass-through firms have higher operating costs.

Dr. Jalbert continued this work, comparing 94 master limited partnerships against samples of C corporations matched to industry and size in one control group and risk factors (using betas) in a second control group, examining only no-growth firms, a significant underlying control factor.

Dr. Jalbert found a significant difference in the value per dollar of net operating income of the pass-through firms compared to the double-taxed firms. He also found that, as debt in the capital structure of the double-taxed firm rose, the valuation difference decreased. Finally, he found that double-taxed firms use more debt in their capital structure than pass-through firms (a finding confirmed by *Pratt's Stats* transaction data). From this, Dr. Jalbert concluded that "the method by which the firm is taxed affects the value of the firm as well as the capital structure the firm will adopt.... [Pass-through firms] have a higher value per dollar of [net operating income] than [double-taxed firms] ... the differential in value is mitigated among firms that use higher levels of debt."

This study contributed to the literature by finding that the extent of debt in the capital structure of pass-through firms versus double-taxed firms affects the value determination. As noted in Appendix A, this is an area that warrants further research.

Research by Merle Erickson, associate professor of accounting at the University of Chicago Graduate School of Business, published in *Capital Ideas*, Vol. 3, No. 3, Winter 2002.

Dr. Erickson compared purchase prices across sets of taxable stock acquisitions of S and free-standing C corporations. His research found that tax benefits in S corporation acquisitions (specifically, 338(h)(10) elections) can total 12% to 17% of the deal's value and that target company shareholders often capture these benefits in the form of a higher purchase price.

As noted earlier, the potential benefits of an IRC Section 338(h)(10) election has been largely absent from the S corp discussion. While circumstances under which such an election may be made are limited (generally) to an acquisition of greater than 80% of the company (by vote and by value), when it is available, it can be substantial. It is important to understand that Dr. Erickson's study did not address the question of difference in value between subchapter C corporations and pass-through entities, only on the value of the step up in basis.

Study of *Pratt's Stats* database by Michael J. Mattson, MBA; Donald S. Shannon, Ph.D., CPA; and David E. Upton, Ph.D., CFA, published in *Shannon Pratt's Business Valuation Update*, November 2002.

This study reviewed over 1,200 each of S and C corporations in the *Pratt's Stats* database (after eliminating those that did not distinguish). This was the largest study to date on comparative prices. However, it made no distinction between asset sales and stock sales.

The study found that, on unadjusted basis, controlling only for size, C corporations sold for more than S corporations based on the mean transaction data. The researchers then made adjustments for:

1. The effects of industry affiliation;
2. Whether the transaction was an asset or stock sale;
3. Any unusual effects stemming from asset size; and
4. The effects of market swings.

After adjustments, the study found no discernible difference in the values of C corporations versus S corporations.

The study was updated and published in the December 2002 edition of *Business Valuation Update*. This update was largely in reaction to the study done by Dr. Erickson.

Here, the researchers replicated the earlier study but performed statistical analysis of stock sales only. Regression results for the two largest size categories—the only size category Erickson used—showed S corporations having higher price-to-sales ratios than C corporations. However, when considering all 17 size categories, no such statement can be made. In fact, in all but one category, the mean C corp multiples were greater than S corporation multiples.

The Financial Resources Management Inc. study by Joseph D. Vinso, Ph.D., MCBA, FIBA, ASA, published in *Valuation Strategies* in the September/October 2003 edition.

This study utilized data from Standard Industrial Code 5411 of Business Valuation Resources' database (*Pratt's Stats*). It examined mean price-to-sales ratios for S corporations versus C corporations. It also made a distinction for limited liability companies, partnerships, and sole proprietorships.

Based on sales multiples, the study found that C corporations are valued higher than S corporations.

"S Corp or C Corp? M&A Deal Prices Look Alike" by John R. Phillips of Marshall and Stevens was published in *Shannon Pratt's Business Valuation Update* in March 2004.

This study analyzed 2,305 stock and asset transactions of S and C corporations in the *Pratt's Stats* database. This was the first study to stratify:

- S corp stock versus C corp stock sale; and
- S corp asset versus C corp asset sale.

The study found no discernible difference in the pricing of S corporation versus C corporation sales, regardless of whether asset or stock sales. It additionally found that total asset transactions are priced at a 20% discount compared to stock transactions.

The results of these studies are mixed but generally find no meaningful differential between S corporation and C corporation pricing, except in the case where a 338(h)(10) election was made.

Note that, with the exception of the study by Dr. Erickson (which largely focused on large companies), as much as anything, these studies may provide an indication that C corporations mimic the benefits of pass-through entities, at least for smaller C corporations. Initial research has shown this to be the case. As noted in Appendix A, this is an area where further research is warranted.

Our study. To further this research, we performed our own large sample study of transactions involving the sale of U.S. commercial banks. Banks provide an ideal sample for comparing the sale of C corporations and S corporations for several reasons. First, they are heavily regulated and thus have similar levels of capital, asset composition, etc. This commonality lessens the chance that unidentified, company-specific factors may drive observed differences in transaction values. Second, virtually all bank transactions, involving both S corporations and C corporations, are stock sales. Third, while the vast majority of U.S. commercial banks are not publicly traded, virtually all are professionally managed and have uniform and comprehensive accounting and financial reporting requirements. Moreover, all financial information is publicly available, even for closely held banks. Finally, both sellers and buyers of U.S. commercial banks are generally sophisticated and well-financed parties. The availability of high-quality financial information, combined with a large number of transactions between well-informed buyers and sellers, provides an ideal test of differences in transaction prices between banks operating as C corporations and S corporations.

Prior to 1997, U.S. commercial banks were not eligible for subchapter S elections. However, with passage of the Small Business Job Protection Act of 1996, commercial banks were allowed to make the election. According to Federal Reserve data, by June 2000, 1,425 commercial banks (approximately 20%) had converted to S corporation status.

Since 1997, the U.S. commercial banking industry has experienced a large number of mergers, acquisitions, and other control transactions. According to the FDIC, at the end of 1997, there were 9,143 commercial banks. Between that time and the end of 2014, there were a total of 1,692 new bank formations, 546 bank failures, and 4,710 bank mergers. In addition to this large number of mergers, there were several thousand sales of controlling interests in banks in nonmerger transactions. In short, this level of activity provides a very large sample of similar transactions.

To examine the impact of tax status (subchapter C versus subchapter S) on sales price, we test the following null hypothesis:

> H1: Tax status of the acquired company (subchapter C versus subchapter S) has no impact on the purchase/sales price of U.S. commercial banks acquired by all buyers.

Large, publicly traded banks purchased a large number of the banks. Since such buyers have no way to avail themselves of any future tax benefits of an acquired S corporation, including them in our study may bias our findings. Thus, we modify our study to test the following null hypothesis by limiting our transactions to banks acquired by non-publicly traded banks:

> H2: Tax status (subchapter C versus subchapter S) has no impact on the purchase/sales price of U.S. commercial banks acquired by non-publicly traded buyers.

To test these hypotheses, we collected data on 2,347 bank sales taking place between Jan. 1, 1997, and Dec. 31, 2008. The screening process utilized to create a homogeneous sample of relevant transactions is summarized as follows:

- Start with all completed commercial bank transactions (excludes government-assisted transactions, excludes sales of savings banks and thrifts). Only whole entity transactions (100% sale of stock) are included.
- Banks could not elect sub S until 1997, and, by June 2000, 18% of community banks (the banks we will be studying) had elected subchapter S. Our study was limited to bank sales completed after 1996.
- The Great Recession officially began in December of 2007 and bank M&A activity collapsed in 2008 and 2009. Virtually all bank transactions during that period were troubled bank acquisitions with or without FDIC assistance. Bank M&A activity resumed in 2010, but pricing of public bank stocks and M&A deals bear little resemblance to pre-2008 deals. Since inclusion of post-2008 transactions would create a less homogeneous sample of transactions, we limit our study to pre-2008 transactions.
- When nonprofitable banks and/or banks with relatively large amounts of nonperforming assets such as delinquent loans or repossessed real estate (OREO) are sold, transaction prices generally reflect substantial unobservable

operating factors related to the eventual disposition of bad loans, OREO, etc. Such factors would be evaluated as part of the due diligence of the buyer, and thus impounded in transaction price, but are unobservable to us. Additionally, tax benefits of NOLs may be priced into the observed sales prices. Thus, we removed all transactions involving the sale of a bank: (1) that had operating losses at the time of sale or was only marginally profitable (return on assets less than 0.1%); or (2) reported total nonperforming assets (as defined by the FDIC) of more than 4% of total assets.

- Although there is no statutory limitation on the size of a subchapter S company, there are limitations to the number of shareholders and access to capital. Thus, it is logical that larger banks will be much less likely to elect subchapter S than small banks, creating a correlation between size and tax status. Since size is also directly related to value, we avoid correlation between size and tax status by limiting the size of the acquired banks to those with assets of less than $1.1 billion. The largest electing subchapter S bank meeting all of our selection criteria reported assets of $1.097 billion, so we view this as the upper size limit for sub S elections. Including banks sales larger than this would provide no additional evidence on the relative values.

- Regulatory capital requirements are critical to banks and create a nonlinear relationship between capitalization and value, especially at the low end. To limit our observations to a linear range, we retain in the sample only acquired banks with equity-to-asset ratios between 20% and 6%.

Using these selection criteria, a total of 2,055 bank transactions were included in our test of H1. To determine the impact of tax status on bank transaction values, a regression model was constructed using actual sales price as the dependent variable. Independent variables included fundamental, company-specific value drivers including total assets (a measure of size), capital to assets (a measure of capitalization), return on assets (profitability), nonperforming assets divided by total assets (a measure of asset and earnings quality), and core deposits divided by total deposits (a measure of deposit liability cost and stability). Because market prices of publicly traded stocks should impact their cost of capital and by extension prices paid by those banks, the KBW public bank index value for the transaction date was also included as a control variable.[128]

128 The KBW Index is named after Keefe, Bruyette and Woods, a recognized authority in the banking industry. It is an economic index consisting of the stocks of 24 banking companies, which serves as a benchmark of the banking sector. The index trades on the Philadelphia Stock Exchange.

Two indicator (dummy) variables were also included. The tax status of the acquired bank was included as an indicator variable coded as "1" if the bank was a subchapter S election at the time of the sale, "0" if not. Similarly, all transactions were coded with a "1" if the acquiring bank was a publicly traded bank. The expected sign of the relationship of each independent variable with prices paid is outlined in Exhibit D-1.

Exhibit D-1. Relationship of Each Independent Variable With Prices Paid	
Independent Variable Description	**Expected Sign**
Tax status (S corporate status, yes or no?)*	+
Buyer is public company (yes or no)?	+
Total assets $	+
Capital/total assets %	+
Return on total assets %	+
Core deposit/total deposits %	+
Nonperforming assets/total assets %	-
Bank stock index	+

*According to the Tax Court, the subchapter S indicator variable should have a significant, positive coefficient with a value of approximately 0.50% of the mean price paid for the sample of banks.

Results of the regression are shown in Exhibit D-2. As shown in Exhibit D-2, all of the control variables are significant with the anticipated sign. Moreover, the overall model is highly significant with an adjusted R^2 of 87.59 and a highly significant *F* value of 1,812 (significant at the 0.001 level). In short, the overall regression results indicate a robust model for the transaction prices of U.S. community banks.

Exhibit D-2. Regression Results: Dollar Price Paid as Dependent Variable				
Independent Variable	**Expected Sign**	**Coefficient**	**T-Stat**	**P-value**
Tax status	+	(4,310.86)	(2.00)	0.0459
Buyer public	+	2,738.37	3.31	0.0009
Assets $	+	0.22	113.75	0.0000
Capital/assets %	+	1,101.70	6.73	0.0000
ROA %	+	9,528.53	12.07	0.0000
Core deposits %	+	129.18	3.18	0.0015
NPA %	-	(1,541.47)	(2.66)	0.0079
Bank stock index	+	70.19	2.49	0.0128

The key variable of interest, tax status, was only significant at the 0.05 level of confidence, indicating that it had a much weaker relationship with prices paid than the other variables. More importantly, the tax status had a negative coefficient. This indicates that subchapter S banks actually sold for a discount rather than a premium.

As a means of deriving a more meaningful measure for the variable of interest, the dependent variable (price paid) was scaled by book value and the resulting price-to-book ratio was used as the dependent variable. The results for this regression are shown in Exhibit D-3.

Exhibit D-3. Regression Results: Price to Book Value as Dependent Variable

Independent Variable	Expected Sign	Coefficient	T-Stat	P-value
Tax status	+	-0.175	-2.545	0.011
Buyer public	+	0.310	11.722	0.000
Assets $	?	0.000	7.358	0.000
Capital/assets %*	-	-0.104	-19.770	0.000
ROA %	+	0.434	16.835	0.000
Core deposits %	+	0.004	2.772	0.006
NPA %	-	-0.116	-6.303	0.000
Bank stock index	+	0.002	2.328	0.020

*Note that the expected sign of the coefficient for capital/assets was positive when price paid was the dependent variable. Because the banks, on average, traded at a price more than twice book value, price to book value will normally decrease as level of capitalization increases. Thus, the sign is negative for this regression. The expected sign for total assets (size) is now uncertain.

The arithmetic mean price to book value for the sample was 210%. With a significant coefficient of negative 0.175, it appears that the subchapter S election was associated with an 8.33% lower sales price (0.175/2.10). This finding is in sharp contrast with the Tax Court's decisions concluding that subchapter S results in a significant (as much as 67%) premium in fair market value.

It is important to note that the public buyer coefficient is also positive and highly significant, indicating that prices paid for acquisitions by publicly traded banks (regardless of form of entity) were significantly higher.

If public banks pay higher acquisition prices, and tend to buy C corporations rather than S corporations, this could explain the negative coefficient for the tax variable found above. Thus, we removed all such transactions, allowing us to focus on the remaining 997 transactions in which a private individual or nonpublic entity purchased a nonpublic bank. These transactions should represent those where both buyers and sellers could, conceivably, utilize a subchapter S election and receive the financial benefits of that election. If there are enhancements to value from the election, it would most likely be found using this sample. Once again, using price to book as the dependent variable, the regression results Exhibit D-4 were obtained.

All control variables were highly significant with the expected signs, and the model produced an adjusted R^2 of 26.68%. Once again, the variable of interest (tax status)

Exhibit D-4. Regression Results: Price to Book Value as Dependent Variable, No Public Buyers				
Independent Variable	Expected Sign	Coefficient	T-Stat	P-value
Tax status (dummy)	+	(0.159)	(1.974)	0.049
Assets $	+	0.000	8.789	0.000
Capital/assets %	-	(0.083)	(11.505)	0.000
ROA %	+	0.384	11.059	0.000
Core dep %	+	0.003	1.695	0.090
NPA %	-	(0.096)	(4.137)	0.000

was barely significant at the 0.05 level of confidence with a negative coefficient. Given the mean price to book value for this sample of 1.90, the 0.159 coefficient is not only statistically significant but economically significant. In short, subchapter S banks have systematically sold for less than nonelecting banks, even when purchased by nonpublic companies.

Such a finding has no theoretical underpinning from a tax perspective. However, one should keep in mind that the sample banks were not randomly allocated tax status. Theory suggests that owners will make a subchapter S election, or forego it, based on a number of shareholder-specific attributes (including shareholder tax rates) as well as company-specific attributes such as anticipated dividend policy and growth potential. It is possible that the negative coefficient is not a reflection of tax status but of the factors that impact the decision to elect subchapter S in the first place.

Empirical data support this theory. Two senior analysts at the Federal Reserve, James Harvey and Jane Padget, noted systematic differences in fundamentals between banks making subchapter S elections and those that did not:

> Banks that have been slow growing and/or expect to be slow growing in the future usually have less need to retain earnings and are more likely to pay higher dividends. Therefore, banks that have converted to subchapter S should exhibit slower asset growth rates both before and after conversion than nonsubchapter S banks. In all four asset growth comparisons, the subchapter S banks grew at substantially slower rates than the nonsubchapter S banks.[129]

129 James Harvey and Jane Padget, "Subchapter S - A New Tool for Enhancing the Value of Community Banks," Federal Reserve Bank of Kansas City, Financial Industry Perspectives, 2000. www.kansascityfed.org/PUBLICAT/FIP/prs00-2.pdf.

According to their analysis, shareholders elect subchapter S when the bank is facing a low-growth environment, does not need additional capital, and will thus be making substantial dividends. In that situation, a Subchapter S election will allow avoidance of a double tax, thus maximizing value to the shareholders. What is implicit in their analysis is that nonelecting banks are also maximizing value to the shareholders by not making the election.

Shareholders of nonelecting banks represent a clientele that is seeking (and valuing) growth over dividends. They can avoid the double tax by simply not distributing dividends and deferring sales of stock, simultaneously avoiding shareholder-level taxes while increasing growth in value. In such a situation, there would be no benefit to a subchapter S election. Given the observations of Harvey and Padget, the observed negative coefficient for tax status most likely captures the low-growth position, and thus lower value, of the subchapter S electors.

What are the implications for the pass-through entity premium? It is quite possible that the tax status variable is simultaneously capturing a negative effect from low anticipated growth and a positive effect from the subchapter S election. However, even if this is the case, it is highly unlikely that a large tax-related premium (such as is calculated by the no tax affect model) could be reduced to an 8% discount through this combination of factors.

Appendix E. Digests of Cases Addressing Pass-Through Entity Issues

Table of Cases in Alphabetical Order			
Case Name	**Date**	**State/Jurisdiction**	**Page**
Estate of Adams v. Commissioner	March 28, 2002	Federal	106
Bank of America, N.A. v. Veluchamy (In re Veluchamy)	December 18, 2015	Federal	138
Bernier v. Bernier	June 29, 2012	Massachusetts	128
Dallas v. Commissioner	September 28, 2006	Federal	113
Delaware Open MRI Radiology Associates, P.A. v. Kessler	April 26, 2006	Delaware	123
Estate of Gallagher v. Commissioner	June 28, 2011	Federal	117
Estate of Giustina v. Commissioner	December 5, 2014	Federal Circuit	132
Gross v. Commissioner	November 19, 2001	Federal/6th Circut	97
Hamelink v. Hamelink	Dec. 30, 2013/ Feb. 26, 2014	Minnesota	135
Estate of Heck v. Commissioner	February 5, 2002	Federal	109
Wall v. Commissioner	March 27, 2001	Federal	101

Editor's note: A full court opinion for each case digested in this section can be found at www.bvlibrary.com.

■ *Gross v. Commissioner*, T.C. Memo 1999-254, aff'd 272 F.3d 333 (6th Cir. 2001)

In a federal gift tax dispute over the value of a minority stock ownership interest in the taxpayers' S corporation, the central issue in front of the Tax Court (J. Halpern) was whether the taxpayers could deduct a "fictitious" corporate tax, that is, the amount of taxes that would be due if the company were organized as a C corporation, when calculating the fair market value of the gifted interest in a pass-through entity under the income approach. The court found they could not and upheld the Service's valuation.

Background. In 1992, two members, and their spouses, belonging to a family that owned a successful beverage bottling and distribution business in Ohio, transferred shares of common stock in the company to their respective children. Each of the gifts represented less than a 1% interest in the corporation. The company had S corp status, which the shareholders of the company agreed to maintain. They also made an agreement restricting the transfer of company shares by and among members of the family. From 1988 through 1992, there was a steady increase in the company's operating income, total income, and distributions to shareholders. Distributions almost equaled the company's total income. Relying on appraisals from a business valuation firm, the taxpayers used a value of $5,680 per share when reporting gift tax on Form 706, United States Gift (and Generation Skipping Transfer) Tax Return.

The IRS initially claimed each share was worth over $11,700 but subsequently lowered the value to $10,910. The taxpayers petitioned the Tax Court for a redetermination of the fair market value of minority interests in the company's common stock.

Parties' expert testimony. At trial, the taxpayers relied on two experts—the second expert was a rebuttal expert—and the government presented one expert.

1. *Taxpayers' first expert.* The taxpayers' first expert used three methods to determine the per-share value: market price comparison approach, discounted future free cash-flow analysis (DFFCF), and capitalization of earnings approach. He weighted the results of the second and third methods equally and assigned only one-third of the weight to the value resulting from the first analysis. Applying a 35% discount for lack of marketability (DLOM), he arrived at the $5,680 a share value.

A critical component of his DFFCF analysis was his applying an assumed 40% corporate tax rate to the future stream of income from the company before discounting the earnings to present value. He called this approach "tax affecting" and maintained that it conformed to the standards governing the conduct of professional business appraisers whose responsibility it was to produce a credible result. It sought to offset possible future tax burdens, such as distributions to shareholders that were insufficient to cover their tax obligations or the risk that the company might lose its favorable S corp status.

As for the DLOM, he said that various studies considering the lack of marketability of closely held and restricted securities suggested a 30% rate for shares that would eventually become freely tradable. However, because the shares of the company at issue were illiquid and not marketable, a 35% rate was appropriate.

He also calculated a 19% cost of capital, explaining that this rate fell within the range of yields to maturity for very small capitalization companies. He explained that he had cross-checked his conclusion by using the build-up method (BUM) to determine the required rate of return.

2. *IRS expert.* The IRS's expert also calculated the value per share with a discounted cash-flow analysis (DCF) but used a comparable companies analysis to test his conclusions. Although his income approach was similar to that of the taxpayers' expert, his analysis yielded a per-share value that was almost double that proposed by the opposing experts.

A critical difference between the valuations was that he used a 0% corporate tax rate. He knew the company was an S corp and assumed it likely would maintain that status indefinitely. Based on its historical distributions, he also assumed the company would continue to distribute most of its earnings to the shareholders. Because income taxes passed through to the company's shareholders and were taken into account in computing their tax liabilities, he determined there should be no reduction in determining corporate earnings available for distribution. He did not consider shareholder-level taxes in calculating his discount rate.

He proposed a 25% DLOM based largely on his "own empirical analysis" of DLOM and factors specific to the company, including its generous dividend distribution policy and greater marketability restrictions.

He arrived at a 14.4% weighted cost of capital by using a 15.5% cost of equity and an 8.25% cost of debt. He generated the cost of equity by way of the capital asset pricing model (CAPM).

3. *Taxpayers' rebuttal expert.* The taxpayers' rebuttal—second—expert specifically rejected the 0% corporate tax rate assumption. He argued that a valuation relying on it failed to account for the known payment of taxes:

> Whether the outflow is a cash distribution made by an S corporation to satisfy shareholders' tax liability, or the direct payment of a tax liability by a C corporation, the decrease in cash experienced by either entity represents a known payment which reduces the availability of cash which could otherwise be used to maintain or expand existing operations. Such a decrease must be taken into consideration when valuing an entity, whether it is structured as a C corporation or an S corporation.

4. *Taxpayers' additional evidence.* In addition, the taxpayers argued that their valuations relied on two internal IRS documents—a valuation guide for income, estate, and gift taxes, as well as a handbook for estate tax examiners—that mandated tax affecting when applying a DCF analysis to establish the value of an S corp.

Taxpayers' failed *Daubert* motion. The taxpayers first challenged the IRS expert's testimony in a *Daubert* motion arguing principally that he used an unreliable method and that his underlying data and empirical analysis were not properly peer reviewed.

The court swiftly dismissed the arguments. For one, the expert had used a DCF analysis, a method the taxpayers' own expert used. "When properly applied, a discounted cash-flow analysis is a reliable tool for financial analysis," the court stated. Also, since the parties merely disagreed over factors and assumptions figuring into the calculations, the court refused to consider the peer review argument. It found the expert's testimony was admissible.

Court credits IRS expert's analysis. At the outset of its analysis, the court noted that tax affecting—whether or not to do it—was the main reason for the considerable difference in the parties' proposed values.

The court flat out rejected the taxpayers' attempt to bolster their position in favor of tax affecting by citing the IRS documents. The court did not interpret the documents to require tax affecting when using a DCF analysis to value an S corp. But even if that is what they meant, the court found that the documents lacked authority since they were neither regulations nor rulings. Further, the taxpayers failed to show that they relied on either document for their valuations.

Similarly, the court found none of the arguments the taxpayers' experts made in favor of tax affecting was persuasive. The court said that theoretically speaking it was not appropriate to tax affect to offset a potential tax burden linked to S corp status. More concretely, in this case, the company had stable growth and a history of paying out dividends that almost equaled its entire income. Also, there was no evidence that the company's corporate status would change.

As for the rebuttal expert's argument that the IRS expert failed to consider "the known payment of taxes," the court said it was unclear whether the rebuttal expert meant the avoided corporate tax applying to a C corp or the shareholder-level tax. Assuming he meant the corporate tax, the expert failed to provide a good reason why the IRS expert should have applied a "hypothetical corporate tax rate in excess of the zero-percent actual corporate tax rate he did apply." According to the court, a hypothetical corporate tax was an insufficient substitute "for certain difficult to quantify disadvantages" accompanying S corp status. The court continued: "We believe the principal benefit that shareholders expect from an S corporation election is a reduction in the total tax burden imposed on the enterprise ... and we see no reason why that savings ought to be ignored as a matter of course in valuing the S corporation."[130]

Further, the court dismissed the proposition that a present-value analysis required tax affecting to account for shareholder-level taxes. If the taxpayers' expert assumed the IRS's expert ignored shareholder-level taxes, the taxpayers' expert was wrong. The IRS expert knew the shareholders would incur the taxes but disregarded them in projecting the company's available cash and the appropriate discount rate. According to the court, "[i]f, in determining the present value of any future payment, the discount rate is assumed to be an after-shareholder-tax rate of return, then the cash-flow should be reduced (tax affected) to an after-shareholder-tax amount. If, on the other hand, a pre-shareholder-tax discount rate is applied, no adjustment for taxes should be made to the cash-flow."[131] Here, the IRS's expert assumed a pre-shareholder-tax discount rate and, therefore, did not err in failing to tax affect the expected cash flow.

The Tax Court also adopted the IRS expert's DLOM and cost of capital determinations. Accordingly, it found the per-share value of the company on the gift date was $10,910.

■ *Wall v. Commissioner,* T.C. Memo 2001-75

In a dispute over the federal gift tax liability arising out of the taxpayers' transfer of stock of a family corporation into trusts benefitting the taxpayers' children, the Tax Court (J. Beghe) adopted the value per share appearing in the Internal Revenue Service's notice of deficiency. Although the parties presented expert reports for trial, the court found the experts' calculations resulting from both market and income approaches unreliable. Tax affecting was among the flaws the court noted in the income-based analyses both sides' experts performed.

130 *Authors' note:* The tax court acknowledges that it is a *reduction in the total tax burden* that the shareholders expect in an S corporation. The court goes on, however, not to reflect a reduction in the tax burden but rather to *eliminate the entire tax burden* of the S corporation. The benefit of a reduction in the total tax burden would not be the total elimination of it but rather an adjustment for the difference in the tax burden of a public C corporation versus the S corporation. This distinction has the effect of significantly overvaluing the S corporation.

131 *Author's note:* As of the writing of this guide, no court has been presented evidence that demonstrates that the discount rate is affected by shareholder taxes. It is that evidence which this book seeks to address, by presenting the evidence of the effect of taxes on value.

Background. The taxpayers transferred 9,380 shares of nonvoting stock in an S corporation to 20 trusts for the benefit of their 10 children on Jan. 1, 1992. The company was a national direct mail distributor and office supply manufacturer in Wisconsin. For the five years prior to the gifts, the company showed a steady increase in revenues but a decrease in net income. Declining profitability was attributable to increases in marketing and administrative expenses. Management predicted that net income would return to historic levels in 1992, notwithstanding unfavorable economic conditions.

Six months prior to the gifts, the company sold its media division. The assets were worth $1.2 million; the company received $120,000 in cash and a "media note" for the remaining $1.08 million. The note bore interest at 7.64%.

Between 1978 and the 1992 valuation date, six transactions of company stock took place. Three of the transactions occurred more than five years prior to the valuation date, and three took place two years before the gifts. The three transactions were redemptions of the company's voting stock from three of its officers; the redemption price exceeded book value by about 8%.

On their gift tax returns, the taxpayers stated the fair market value (FMV) of the stock was $221.75 per share. The IRS issued notices of deficiency, claiming the value was $260.13 per share. The difference in value at that stage in the dispute was only about 17%. Regardless, the parties were unable to settle their disagreements and the taxpayers petitioned the Tax Court for a determination of the fair market value of the company stock.

Taxpayers' expert's opinions. The taxpayers' gift tax return value was based on a report their expert had prepared several years before trial. The analysis relied almost entirely on the guideline public company approach based on historical performance.

1. *Market-based approach.* The expert first calculated the company's debt-free performance based on earnings before interest and taxes (EBIT), earnings before depreciation, interest, and taxes (EBDIT), debt-free net income (DFNI), debt-free cash flow (DFCF), and debt-free book value. In determining the measures, she excluded income attributable to the media division because of its sale in 1991. She then selected seven comparable public companies and determined their multiples of the selected performance measures. She selected the multiples based on three of the companies that had suffered declining earnings rather than based on the mean of the entire group. Applying her multiplies to the earnings measures, she found the company's total invested capital had a value of approximately $10.6 million. Deducting debt, she calculated that the value of its equity was $4.9 million on a marketable minority basis.

The expert also applied the guideline public company method to the company's projected earnings for 1992, the year of the gifts. Based on the projections, she calculated the EBIT, EBDIT, and after-tax earnings of the company. She applied multiples from two of the previously selected comparable companies to the forecasted earnings. Under this approach, the company's value of equity, as if publicly traded, was almost $4.9 million. After applying a 40% discount for lack of marketability (DLOM) and a 5% discount for nonvoting stock to the equity values determined under each calculation, she arrived at an FMV of $211.20 per share.

2. *Income approach.* In response to criticism from the IRS that she had failed to provide an income-based calculation, the expert subsequently prepared a revised report. She first calculated the company's future cash flow using the company's historical results to develop a "normalized" free cash flow, which she assumed would grow 5% per year indefinitely after 1992. Importantly, her adjustments included subtracting hypothetical income taxes at a rate of 34%. She concluded that normalized cash flow for the valuation year would be $720,317. To calculate the appropriate capitalization rate, she considered the 1991 yield on 30-year Treasury bonds and data from the *1992 Ibbotson Yearbook.* She added an equity risk premium, a small-stock risk premium, and a company-specific risk premium and arrived at a rate of 22.75%. She also applied a 40% DLOM and a 5% nonvoting stock discount and determined that the value of the stock under the income approach was considerably less—$175.24 per share.

The expert's revised report gave equal weight to the values resulting from the market-based and income-based analyses and concluded that the stock was worth $192.20 per share, thus less than the value appearing in the original report.

IRS expert's valuations. Similarly, the IRS's expert used market and income approaches to value the company's shares.

1. *Market-based approach.* The IRS expert relied on the opposing expert's determinations of the company's net revenues and net incomes for the years preceding the valuation date as a starting point for his performance measures. He also used two of the rivaling expert's guideline companies. On the whole, however, he used far fewer of the performance measures and guideline companies than she had to generate the company's value.

Critically, he treated the media note as a separate, nonoperating asset. He calculated four performance measures including the adjusted net income. He next selected three comparable public companies. Using these measures, he calculated the value of the company's equity and applied a 40% DLOM and only a 2% discount for nonvoting stock, arriving at an FMV for nonvoting stock of $303.03 per share.

2. *Income approach.* The expert's income approach relied on a discounted cash-flow analysis. He projected the company's operating results for the five years after the valuation. Just as the opposing expert, he tax affected the company's earnings, but, instead of 34%, he used a 40% tax rate. He calculated a 15% discount rate based on the rate of long-term Baa-rated corporate bonds and used a 6% company-specific risk rate. He also increased the discount rate by half a percent for the next four years and used a 17% discount rate for the terminal rate. He next added the present value of the cash flows and the terminal value and applied a 17% minority interest discount. Finally, he added the face value of the media note and applied a 40% DLOM and a 2% nonvoting stock discount. He concluded that the value was $260.61 per share, slightly higher than the value appearing in the notices of deficiency. For the final valuation, he accorded the value resulting from the income-based analysis twice the weight of the value from the market-based calculation. This weighting yielded a $273.99-per-share value.

Court rejects prior transactions as indicators of value. At the start of its discussion, the Tax Court pointedly observed that the difference in the parties' original positions was small enough for them to settle the matter outside the courtroom, which they opted not to do. On the other hand, litigation "has driven the parties further apart."

The Tax Court found none of the six prior transactions were "the best evidence" of the stock's FMV. The first three events were too distant from the gift, and the last three were different in nature. In all instances, the stock was subject to buy-sell agreements, stipulating that the purchase price was the book value of the stock on the date the employee was terminated, died, or retired. However, the redemptions did not follow the buy-sell agreements. The court also noted that the corporation had experienced two additional years of declining net profits between the date of the sale and the valuation date.

The Tax Court found flaws in the valuations of both experts. With respect to the guideline public company analyses, the court preferred the IRS expert's treatment of the media note as a nonoperating asset. On the other hand, it accepted the taxpayers' expert's argument in favor of a 25% minority discount "because a minority stockholder could not require liquidation of [the company] and thus could not realize the note's full value." It also determined that the taxpayers' expert had made transcription errors in calculating the forecast earnings of the company, which contributed to a "significant" understatement of the company's value. Moreover, the expert's choice of multiples was incorrect. The court noted that her use of the lower multiples did not align with her claim that the company's risk levels and profitability were close to the industry norm after considering the decline in profitability of the company.

The court faulted the IRS's expert for using too few performance measures and noted that his choice of multiples varied from company to company and begged for an explanation.

The Tax Court also rejected the values resulting from the experts' income-based analyses. Valuation literature taught that "if the subject company's future income is unpredictable, then income-based methods will produce inaccurate appraisals." Here, there were no long-term management projections available. Given the past fluctuations in the company's profits and the economic conditions in the industry on the valuation date, it was difficult to predict the company's future performance based on historical performance. The taxpayers' expert sought to circumvent the problem by developing "normalized" free cash flow, but a leading treatise on business valuations cautioned that "an analyst should use such averages only if she can explain why they are a reasonable proxy for future expectations." The court noted that the IRS's expert's future cash-flow projections were also based in large part on past performance and that he "did not explain or justify very well either his assumptions about future changes in [the company's] performance or his choice of discount rates."

Court notes appraisers disagree over tax affecting. The court commented on both experts' choice to tax affect future cash-flow projections. It pointed out that the taxpayers' expert acknowledged in testimony that there was disagreement in the appraisal community on whether to tax affect the income of an S corp. Those in favor of the practice point out that many potential buyers of S corps are C corps. Because a C corp would be unable to maintain a target company's S corp status following an acquisition, the acquirer would tax affect the S corp's income at C corp rates in deciding how much it would pay for the target. On the other hand, those against the practice emphasize that, even though stockholders of S corps are subject to tax on the corporation's income, they are generally not subject to a second level of tax when that income is distributed to them. Accordingly, an S corp likely is more valuable than an equivalent C corp. However, tax affecting an S corp's income and then determining the value of that income by reference to the rates of return on taxable investments means that an appraisal will give no value to S corp status, the Tax Court observed. This was the methodology the experts followed. "Because this methodology attributes no value to [the company's] S corporation status, we believe it is likely to result in an undervaluation of [the company's] stock," the Tax Court concluded, referencing *Gross v. Commissioner*, T.C. Memo 1999-254.

Court relies on notices of deficiency. The Tax Court noted that there was a presumption that the value of the gifts in the statutory notices of deficiency was correct and that the taxpayers had not met their burden of proving the IRS's original valuation wrong. Accordingly, the value was $260.13 per share.

■ *Estate of Adams v. Commissioner,* T.C. Memo 2002-80

In an estate tax dispute, the estate's expert used the income capitalization approach to determine the fair market value of the decedent's interest in an insurance company that operated as an S corporation. As part of the analysis, he increased the capitalization rate by over 11%, converting it from after corporate tax to before corporate tax to match the tax character of the prospective net cash flows. Although the Tax Court (J. Colvin) credited the estate expert's valuation, citing *Gross v. Commissioner,* it found there was no justification for adjusting the capitalization rate.

Background. The decedent owned 176 shares of voting common stock—a 61.59% interest—in a North Carolina insurance company. The agency was an S corporation since the early 1970s. It functioned both as a retail insurance agency and as the managing general insurance company for Maryland Casualty Co. (MCC). Under the contract with MCC, the company had the exclusive right to sell personal and commercial insurance for MCC in 17 counties in the western part of the state. In 1995, the year the decedent died, around 70% of the company's business came from personal lines. The contract with MCC specified that both parties could terminate their arrangement at any time by giving 180 days' notice. Also, in 1995, litigation was pending that could negatively affect the company, requiring it to pay over $400,000.

The decedent became president of the company in 1972 and worked there up until his death in 1995. At that time, he served as treasurer and his primary responsibility was setting wage and bonus levels for the company's officers. Then, the most important person to the company was its current president, who held 105 shares or a 36.33% interest. He began managing the company in the early 1980s and understood all aspects of underwriting. He cultivated close relationships with independent agents who sold company products and was key to securing the company's relationship with MCC. From 1991 through 1995, there was a steady increase in his salary, from approximately $235,000 to $381,500. His dividends also grew, from about $76,600 in 1991 to $167,200 in 1995.

The decedent's daughter also worked for the company and served as vice president and secretary. She owned six shares or a 2.08% interest in the company. By all accounts, she could not have replaced the president.

Following the decedent's death, a dispute arose between the estate and the IRS over the fair market value (FMV) of the decedent's interest. The estate claimed his interest was worth $920,800. The Service, in turn, valued it at over $1,746,000. Both parties presented expert testimony in front of the Tax Court to support their positions.

Experts agree on approach and discount rates. Both sides' experts relied on an income approach, but the experts used different methods. Neither expert argued that the other's methodology was inappropriate. The IRS's expert performed a discounted cash-flow (DCF) analysis, and the estate's expert used the income capitalization method. Under the DCF, the expert determines and applies a discount rate to a series of future cash-flow periods. Under the income capitalization analysis, he estimates the value of the future cash flow of a single period to which he subsequently applies a capitalization rate. The cap rate combines the estimated growth rate and discount rate.

Here, both experts used the build-up method to calculate the discount rate. They started with the 6.86% risk-free rate based on the 30-year Treasury rate and adjusted it to account for certain risk factors. For example, both added a 7.03% equity risk premium based on the *1995 Ibbotson Yearbook.* They applied a 5.25% small-company risk premium based on data from Ibbotson. The IRS's expert used a 10% risk premium to account for the risk of losing the personal lines of underwriting authority and the company's S corporation status; the estate's expert added a 9.03% risk premium to address the company's uncertain relationship with MCC and its "thin" management and dependence on the company's president.

Experts disagree over cash flow determination. A major disagreement between the experts centered on the calculation of the future net cash flows: specifically, estimating the key employee's future compensation. The IRS agreed that the company's president was a key employee and that no one would buy the company without him. However, its expert argued that the company could have found a replacement for him for $125,000 per year. He derived the figure from looking at the salary of the top 10% of underwriters.

The estate's expert pointed out that the president's total compensation in 1995 was nearly $549,000, including dividends. He considered industry data for officers and managers, which indicated that, for companies with assets of $1 million, officers commanded compensation of 14.6% of gross revenues.

The court credited the estate expert's approach. The evidence showed that few people understood the industry, the market, and the company as well as the president. According to the court, the IRS's expert "ignores the fact that [the president] did much more than underwriting." In fact, underwriting only represented 10% to 15% of his responsibility.

Experts disagree over timing of investor payouts. The IRS's expert also attacked the estate expert's assumption that the company made payouts to investors at the end of the year. This approach "artificially treats net cash flows as not received until the end of the year."

The court disagreed. It found the IRS failed to show the company paid investors in the middle of the year and there was authority supporting the year-end convention: "[P]ayment at the end of the year is better than payment in the middle of the year because payment at the end of the year enables the managers to see how the year has turned out," the court said, referencing Shannon Pratt's *Cost of Capital* (1998).

In general, the court found the estate's expert performed a "more thorough" valuation analysis than the IRS's expert. The latter admitted to not having investigated material facts, including the pending litigation, and thus not being able to determine their effects on the valuation.

Court rejects after-tax capitalization rate. Based on his discount rate and an estimated 6.34% growth rate, the estate's expert calculated a 20.53% capitalization rate, which he subsequently increased to 31.88%. He reasoned that the conversion was necessary to align the after-tax capitalization rate with the before-tax prospective net cash flows.[132]

The court disapproved of the expert's characterization of the net cash flows and the adjustment he made as a consequence. Referencing *Gross v. Commissioner*, the court agreed that "[t]he net cashflow and the capitalization rate used to compute the fair market value of [the company] stock should have the same tax character; i.e., before corporate tax or after corporate tax." However, the court disagreed that in this case the prospective net cash flows were before corporate tax. According to the court, "it is appropriate to use a zero corporate tax rate to estimate net cash flow when the stock being valued is stock of an S corporation."

Here, the subject company was an S corporation and the applicable corporate tax rate was zero. Therefore, the estate's expert's estimates of prospective net cash flows were after corporate tax, as was the 20.53% capitalization rate he originally determined. Since both components matched, converting the capitalization rate to before corporate tax was improper, the court found.

Court discredits experts' DLOM rates. Both experts agreed that a discount for marketability (DLOM) applied but arrived at markedly different rates. The IRS's expert considered restricted stock studies and determined that the average DLOM was between 30% and 35% and that IPO studies indicated a DLOM of nearly 45%. He also reasoned that the company's specialized operations would limit the number of potential buyers; on

132 *Author's note:* Adjusting a discount rate to a pretax level, and then applying it to cash flows that are precorporate income tax, results in the same value as if the after-tax return had been applied to post-corporate tax cash flows. See Exhibit 5-1.

the other hand, the size of the decedent's interest and elements of control could work in favor of marketability. He concluded that a DLOM in the range of 40% to 45% was appropriate.

The estate's expert first calculated a 32.89% discount based on discounts in various restricted stock studies. Because he considered the insurance industry more stable than the general market, he decreased the rate to 20%.

The court agreed a DLOM was appropriate. It disagreed with the estate's expert's decision to lower the rate to 20%, finding the company was not as stable as the industry average. At the same time, it rejected the IRS's expert's increase to 45% "because we believe a 35% discount adequately takes into account [the company's] vulnerabilities."

Modifying the estate's expert's valuation, the Tax Court concluded that the fair market value of the decedent's interest was approximately $1.16 million.

■ *Estate of Heck v. Commissioner*, T.C. Memo 2002-34

In an estate tax dispute, the Tax Court (J. Halpern) rejected the market-based approach to valuing the decedent's minority interest in a unique California champagne producer that operated as an S corporation. The court agreed with both sides' experts that the discounted cash-flow method was the appropriate valuation tool but developed its own analysis incorporating elements from both experts' calculations. It found that a discount for lack of control adequately addressed issues specific to S corporation status.

Background. When the decedent died in 1995, she held 630 shares of stock in F. Korbel and Bros. Inc. (Korbel), then one of the country's premier champagne producers. Her interest amounted to 39.62% of common stock. The company was located in California and operated as an S corporation. In the early 1990s, champagne sales represented about 70% of the company's total sales, brandy sales about 27%, and nonsparkling wine sales about 3%. In 1995, champagne sales made up 95% of gross profits. The Korbel facilities occupied 1,800 acres of land, but 1,099 acres were not in use for business.

Korbel had an agreement with Brown-Forman Corp. (Brown-Forman), under which the latter had worldwide distribution rights for Korbel's champagne and brandy. The contract also gave Brown-Forman the right of first refusal (ROFR) regarding offers of Korbel stock by family members.

On the estate tax return, Form 706, the petitioner, who was the special administrator of the estate, indicated the shares were worth $16,380,000, or $26,000 per share. The

Internal Revenue Service determined a deficiency, claiming the decedent's interest valued $30,177,000, or $47,900 a share.

Both parties presented expert testimony in front of the Tax Court regarding the fair market value of the decedent's interest.

Experts disagree over use of market approach. The IRS's expert used both a market and an income approach for his calculation, weighting the results 30% to 70%, respectively. The market-based analysis relied on the guideline company method. After reviewing over 1,300 companies with an SIC code for wines, brandy, and brandy spirits, he identified only two companies that he said were similar to Korbel: Mondavi and Canandaigua. Ultimately, however, he relied only on multiples from Mondavi and adjusted downwards. Canandaigua was approximately 10 times as big as Korbel in terms of revenue and total assets, it produced many more products than Korbel, and its sparkling wines catered to the low end of the champagne market. The estate's expert objected to the market approach, arguing there was a lack of true comparables. In his rebuttal report, he noted that Mondavi was unique in the way it produced and marketed its wines.

The court found the arguments of the estate's expert persuasive and rejected the guideline company analysis. It said it failed to see how Canandaigua influenced the IRS's expert's calculation and found an analysis based on a single comparable company, Mondavi, unreliable. "A sample of one tells us little about what is normal for the population in question." Moreover, the court pointed out that the IRS did not challenge the estate's expert's claim that Mondavi did not represent the norm.

Court 'deconstructs' experts' DCF analyses to generate its own valuation. As to the income approach, both experts used the discounted cash-flow (DCF) method. But they disagreed about most of the variables making up the framework of the analysis. The Tax Court agreed that the DCF was the appropriate valuation method but found neither expert's valuation was wholly convincing. As a consequence, it was "deconstructing each expert's DCF analysis, and assembling our own."

1. *Cash flow.* Regarding the projected cash flows, the court found the sales growth assumptions the IRS's expert made "more realistic." He determined that sales growth would slow during the projected period from 4.5% in 1995 to 3% in 1999 and thereafter. The court considered this projection in line with the company's compound annual growth rate since 1984, that is, 3.1%.

In contrast, the court adopted the estate's expert's calculation of the company's operating margin (total revenues less cost of goods sold, compensation, deprecation, and other expenses) during the projected period. The expert concluded it was 12% of sales revenues, based on the company's average from the five years preceding the valuation date—1990 to 1994. On the other hand, the IRS's expert computed each cost component using at times a two-year average and other times a five-year average. At the same time, he admitted that in instances where he had selected a two-year average, the opposing expert's consistent use of a five-year rate appeared "reasonable enough." The court found the five-year simple average had "the virtue of consistency." But it adjusted the projected profit margin rate slightly, to 12.3%, to reflect other amounts of small income the estate's expert had included in his rebuttal report.

The court next considered cash-flow adjustments. Both experts added back an amount for depreciation but used a different basis for arriving at the rate. The IRS's expert used a two-year average and projected depreciation at 4% of gross sales, while the estate's expert used a five-year average, yielding a 3.85% rate. The court relied on the five-year average because it generally found the estate's expert's analysis to be more thorough.

The experts also disagreed over the amount of necessary noninventory working capital. While the IRS's expert projected it to be 3.5% of sales, the estate's expert used 5% of sales. The court found this level was based on historical performance and accepted the 5% figure. Finally, the experts disagreed over the amount of projected annual capital expenditures. The court adopted the IRS's expert's calculation: $4 million for 1995 and every year thereafter. It aligned with the average annual $3.8 million in capital expenditures during the relevant precedent five years.

2. *Rate of return.* Both experts calculated the rate of return using the weighted average cost of capital (WACC). The point of contention was the cost of equity capital. Where the estate's expert calculated the cost of equity capital using the capital asset pricing model (CAPM), the IRS's expert used the build-up method. The court noted that neither expert made a strong argument for his position but found the estate's expert's 14.70% was more reasonable than the IRS's expert's 16.71%. It pointed out that the lower the WACC, the higher the present value. Accordingly, the Service had no reason to complain about the court's rejection of the IRS's expert's higher figure.

3. *Present value computation.* Another point of dispute was whether to use a year-end or midyear convention in computing the present value of all cash flow. The court again sided with the estate's expert, who had adopted a year-end convention. Since the champagne-producing and -selling business was highly cyclical and most of Korbel's sales occurred during the last quarter of the year, the year-end convention was more appropriate.

4. *Treatment of nonoperating assets.* Both sides recognized that the company had nonoperating assets consisting of land, insurance proceeds, and a note receivable. The principal disagreement centered on the question of whether the company had excess cash representing a nonoperating asset. Analyzing historical cash levels in relation to gross revenue, the IRS's expert found the company had $5.25 million of cash on the valuation date, which he considered to be a nonoperating asset. The estate's expert concluded there was no excess cash based on information from the majority shareholder about the number of contingencies. The court sided with the estate's expert.

Court considers merit of specific S corp-related discount. A critical point of the discussion concerned the use and rate of various discounts. The estate's expert applied a 25% lack of marketability discount (DLOM) and added an "additional 10 percent to his basic marketability discount." He explained that the latter accounted for the negative effects of the right of first refusal (ROFR) as well as disadvantages related to the decedent's shares representing a minority interest. He called them "agency problems." Adding the two discounts up, the estate's expert generated a 35% "marketability" discount.

In contrast, the IRS's expert applied a 15% "liquidity" discount and a 10% discount specific to S corp-related risks, e.g., uncertainty over whether the S corp will make enough distributions to cover the shareholders' taxes on its earnings and uncertainty over the corporation's favorable tax status. The expert also applied separate 25% DLOMs to nonoperating assets.

The court understood the estate expert's term "marketability" discount and the IRS expert's term "liquidity" discount to mean the same type of discount. It noted that both experts relied on the same studies for the DLOM rate, which suggested a range of 10% to 45%. It found the IRS's expert failed to provide a rationale for choosing the low end of the acceptable range—15%—for a "basic" DLOM. Instead, the court accepted the estate expert's proposed 25% rate.

The court next addressed the issue of accounting for the minority interest or the issue of lack of control (DLOC). Although neither expert expressly used the term "lack of control," the court found the estate's expert's discount for "agency problems" aimed to capture lack of control, as did the IRS's expert's proposed 10% S corp discount. The latter sought to address "several restrictions impairing liquidity." In that connection, the court pointed out that, liquidity problems notwithstanding, the IRS's expert seemed to view S corp status as a benefit but "fail[s] to quantify the relevant advantages and disadvantages."

Both experts also agreed to apply a discount to account for Brown-Forman's ROFR. The IRS's expert included it in his basic 15% DLOM. The estate's expert accounted for it in his additional 10% discount but viewed the ROFR as a more serious threat to marketability than the IRS expert did. According to the estate's expert, the right of first refusal ensured that an outside bidder would have to spend much more time, money, and effort to compete with Brown-Forman in acquiring the decedent's interest. As a result, Brown-Forman's position represented a significant deterrence to outside bidders for the shares, which reduced their value.

Ultimately, the Tax Court adopted the estate's expert's approach. "We are satisfied that some amount of discount is attributable to the ROFR and that 10 percent is an appropriate discount for both the ROFR and the purchaser's minority status, given … [the IRS's expert's] addition of a 10-percent discount for only Korbel's status as an S corporation."

Finally, the court rejected the IRS's expert's application of separate additional discounts for nonoperating assets. Instead, it adopted the estate's expert's approach to apply a combined 35% marketability discount to all the operating and nonoperating assets of the company. "We see no reason to limit a minority discount to particular assets of Korbel even if they are nonoperating assets and, therefore, more readily available for distribution to shareholders than are Korbel's other operating assets."

Court's value conclusion. The estate's expert arrived at a value of $29,694 per share based on his DCF analysis. This value represented an increase from the $26,000-per-share value the estate had stated in Form 706. The court considered the change in position a concession. The IRS adhered to the value in the deficiency notice, $47,900 per share, even though its expert's direct testimony indicated a slightly higher valuation.

The court's own DCF analysis yielded a fair market value of $32,174 per share.

■ *Dallas v. Commissioner*, T.C. Memo 2006-212

A number of critical facts in this gift tax dispute resemble the facts in *Gross v. Commissioner*, as does the outcome regarding tax affecting. Here, the Tax Court (J. Colvin) dismissed the petitioner's effort to distinguish its case from *Gross* by arguing the company at issue distributed a different proportion of earnings to shareholders than the company in *Gross*. The court found this difference to be irrelevant and soundly rejected tax affecting for S corporations.

Background. The petitioner-father held the stock in an S corporation that manufactured ammonium chloride and magnesium silicate and distributed the chemicals in the United States and around the world. The company's headquarters were in New Jersey. The petitioner was chairman of the board, while one son served as president of the company and the other as the company's CEO.

In 1999 and 2000, the father undertook stock transactions that effectively transferred control over the business to his sons. Specifically, in 1999, each son, by way of a trust, received 4,000 nonvoting shares of the business in exchange for $248,000 in cash and a $2,232,000 self-canceling installment note. Additionally, the transaction documents contained a share-adjustment clause. For the 1999 transaction, a third-party appraiser determined the fair market value of the stock was $620 per share based on the capitalization of earnings method. The appraiser's calculation tax affected the stock, using a 40% rate, and applied a 15% discount for lack of control (DLOC) and a 35% discount for lack of marketability (DLOM).

The 2000 transaction was similar, but it involved the transfer of fewer shares and a lesser payment. The parties did not obtain a new appraisal but based the share price on the estimation of the company's CFO. The price was $650 per share.

During an audit, the IRS determined the intrafamily transfers represented gifts. The notes were worth substantially less than their face value because they were self-cancelling. Moreover, the stock price did not reflect the fair market value because of the tax affecting. According to the Service, the petitioner was liable for a $1.7 million deficiency in gift tax for 1999 and for an $823,000 deficiency in 2000. The parties litigated the matter in front of the Tax Court, presenting expert testimony.

Court finds transaction price is not arm's-length price. The Tax Court first addressed the issue of whether the transfers represented arm's-length transactions. It noted that there was a presumption that intrafamily transfers were gifts. Here, the petitioner failed to prove otherwise. The transaction documents contained a share adjustment clause and the note was self-canceling, both attributes that were signs that the transactions were for estate planning purposes. Also, there was no negotiation among the parties and the sons did not retain their own counsel.

Petitioner's tax-affecting arguments fail to resonate with the court. A major disagreement among the experts centered on the question of whether to tax affect. The petitioner presented two appraisers that reduced net income earnings by 40% and 35%, respectively, based on the assumption that the corporation would lose its S corp status after or as a result of the hypothetical sale of its stock. For one, the company could lose its S corp status at any time; secondly, certain potential buyers—C corps—would not qualify to be S corp shareholders.

The Tax Court found this argument unconvincing. There was no evidence that the company expected to change its S corp status. It had a history of making sufficient distributions to shareholders to meet their income tax liabilities. Also, there was no evidence to support the experts' claim that a hypothetical buyer and seller would assume that the S corp would lose its favorable status as a result of the transaction.

The Tax Court gave no credence to the claim that this case differed from the seminal *Gross* case in that in *Gross* the S corp had a consistent annual 100% payout to shareholders, whereas the subject company used retained earnings to expand. In a footnote, the court stated:

> Our analysis [in *Gross*] did not depend on the proportion of corporate income distributed. We said that, in determining the present value of an expected stream of earnings, any tax affecting to reflect the shareholder-level tax burden should be done equally (or not at all) to both the discount rate and the expected cashflows, with the result that, in either case, the present value determined would be the same. That analysis is independent of the proportion of earnings distributed.

Problematic expert testimony undermined the petitioner's position. According to the Tax Court, the petitioner's second appraiser seemed to have lifted passages "verbatim" from the original appraisal and in testimony seemed "substantially unfamiliar" with his own report. Therefore, the opinion deserved "little weight."

The petitioner's original appraisal, which valued the S corp shares at the transfer, also invited the court's criticism. In providing his reasons for tax affecting, the appraiser testified that: (1) he had always tax affected; (2) an informal poll at (an unnamed) conference suggested that 90% to 95% of attendees tax affected; (3) the ASA rejected certification unless applicants tax affected; (4) bankers, investment bankers, and business brokers tax affect S corp sales; and (5) his company had tax affected ESOP valuations for the Department of Labor. Given the vagueness of the statements, the court found this analysis "unpersuasive."

Likewise, the petitioner was unable to convince the court to adopt the Delaware Court of Chancery's tax-affecting rationale in *Delaware Open MRI Radiology Associates, Inc. v. Kessler*, 898 A.2d 290 (Del. Ch. 2006). The Tax Court found the ruling in *Delaware Open MRI* was not applicable in this case because the Delaware case was a dissenting shareholder case that was subject to a fair value standard of value whereas this case was a gift tax matter subject to a fair market value standard of value. The fair market value standard must consider the price a willing hypothetical buyer and seller would negotiate—and, in this case, there was insufficient evidence that the hypothetical parties would tax affect the S corp's earnings.[133] Consequently, tax affecting the company's earnings was "not appropriate."

Court briefly addresses additional discounts. The parties also disagreed on the applicability and rates of certain additional discounts.

1. *Lack of voting power.* Because the petitioner's second appraiser had specifically valued a nonvoting minority interest, he did not apply a DLOC. He did apply a 5% discount for lack of voting power, contending that nonvoting stockholders would not be able to pool their votes as minority shareholders might. Their stock, therefore, was worth less.

The Tax Court disagreed, finding "[a]ny anticipation of minority shareholders' pooling their votes is speculative."

2. *Minority interest.* The petitioner did not dispute the applicability of a 15% minority discount for nonoperating assets but disagreed with the IRS's 20% minority discount for operating assets. He claimed the rate was too low because it resulted from a formula based on the control premium, adjusting for excessive executive compensation.

The Tax Court found "no indication" of this basis and no reason to increase the discount rate.

3. *Lack of marketability.* The petitioner's appraiser reviewed restricted stock studies from several periods, selected the 34.2% mean DLOM from the pre-1990 studies, and increased the rate to 40% to account for the company's weak prospects of going public. In contrast, the IRS's appraiser applied a 20% DLOM.

The court adopted the IRS's expert's rate. It found the petitioner's appraiser used data from the wrong period. Studies from the time in which the transfers took place indicated the median DLOM rate was 13.2%. Therefore, a 20% rate was appropriate.

4. *Fair market value of the notes.* The petitioner had executed the self-canceling notes in 1999; after learning from an IRS reviewer that these provisions reduced the notes' face value, the petitioner deleted those provisions from like notes in the 2000 stock transfer. The petitioner claimed at trial that the 1999 notes had been a "drafting mistake," but

133 *Author's note:* The issue to be addressed is to remove the extent of the tax penalty that exists in the public-market return, so that the discount rate can be properly matched to the income stream (i.e., after corporate taxes). As both standards of value rely on the same methodology for the development of a discount rate, there is no distinction related to tax effects.

the Tax Court held the notes were "unambiguously" self-canceling and their value was less than face value.

Court rejects income adjustment for executive compensation. The IRS's appraiser increased the company's net income based on the assumption that the petitioner and his sons received unreasonably high amounts of compensation that would be reduced in the event of a sale to an unrelated investor.

This contention had no traction with the Tax Court. It found the analysis lacked the quality "customarily used by courts in deciding whether compensation is reasonable." Also, there was no more reason to assume changes in executive compensation policies than there was to assume changes in dividend-paying policies or changes in the company's S corp status.

■ *Estate of Gallagher v. Commissioner*, T.C. Memo 2011-148

In an estate tax dispute involving a minority interest in a private media company, the Tax Court (J. Halpern) addressed many aspects of a private-company valuation. It discussed the appropriate methodology—market versus income approach—and subissues critical to a discounted cash-flow analysis, such as tax affecting, cash-flow projections, and the determination of discounts for lack of control and lack of marketability. The estate's attempt to justify its S corporation-related adjustments by reference to the Tax Court's nonauthoritative (i.e., memorandum decision), anti-tax-affecting *Gross* decision failed.

Background. The decedent owned 15% in a family-founded newspaper publishing company that also owned a television station and a few special media providers. In 1996, the company elected to become an S corporation; a contemporaneous shareholder agreement restricted the sale of stock to protect the S election. Just before the decedent's death on July 5, 2004, the company acquired a 100% interest in another small publishing company. In connection with this and other planned acquisitions, the company refinanced a $400 million debt, for which it prepared certain financial forecasts. Finally, as of the July 5, 2004, valuation date, the company had 2,800 executive stock options outstanding, at an average price of roughly $2,800 per option.

The decedent's federal estate tax return, Form 706, stated the value of her interest at approximately $34.9 million based on an appraisal the company's president and CEO had performed only days after her death. In 2007, the IRS averred the fair market value of the decedent's interest was $49.5 million. The estate petitioned the Tax Court for a redetermination based on a new appraisal at $26.6 million. Before trial, both sides retained different appraisers whose calculations narrowed the value gap. The petitioner then claimed the decedent's units were worth $28.2 million, whereas the IRS valued them at $40.86 million.

Parties' disagreements focus on four areas. The parties' valuation dispute centered on four major categories, which the Tax Court considered in turn.

1. *Date of financial information.* The IRS's expert relied on the company's June 27, 2004, internal financial statements and used second-quarter data (June 30, 2004) for comparable public companies, even though this information was published after the valuation date. In contrast, the estate's expert relied on the latest financial information for both the company and guideline comparable companies that was available before the valuation date (dated March 2004). He reasoned that as of the valuation date a willing buyer and seller would be unaware of the subsequently published information.

The court found the June 2004 data was more appropriate. Just because this information was not publicly available as of the valuation date "is not to say … that our hypothetical actors could not make inquiries of [the company] or of the guideline companies (or of financial analysts), which would have elicited non-publicly available information as to end-of-June conditions." The court also agreed with the IRS's expert's statement that the June 2004 financial data more accurately depicted the market conditions on the valuation date, observing that the estate's expert failed to allege an intervening event that would have caused the June 2004 data to be incorrect.

2. *Adjustments to company's financial statements.* Both experts deducted nonrecurring items from the company's historical financial statements, including a $7.8 million divestiture of assets that occurred in 2000. The estate's expert further deducted $700,000 for a life insurance policy inherited through an acquisition and $1.1 million for self-insurance claims, and he eliminated $11.7 million in pension overfunding. The court accepted the divestiture adjustment but disregarded the other adjustments, pointing out that the estate's expert gave "no explanation" as to why the expenses were recurring and why the overfunded plan did not provide an annual benefit to the company.

3. *Guideline company method (GCM).* Both experts used the GCM, but only the IRS's expert relied on its result, according the GCM value equal weight to the value from the income approach. He selected four companies whose underlying price multiples "generally reflect an investor's assessment of both current and future earnings prospects as well as the business and financial risks, inherent in the Company's business as of the valuation date." In contrast, the estate's expert only used the GCM as a reasonableness check because of the lack of sufficiently comparable publicly held companies.

The court agreed with the estate's expert. It noted that, although the GCM was "generally accepted" for valuing stock of a private company, in this case, only one of the claimed comparables was "arguably" similar enough in size, products, and other aspects to the subject company. "A single company is insufficient on which to base the valuation method," the court said, citing its earlier decision in *Estate of Heck v. Commissioner,* T.C. Memo 2002-34.

4. *Discounted cash-flow (DCF) method.* The court agreed with the estate's appraiser that, in this case, given the lack of comparables, the DCF analysis was "the most appropriate under which to value the units."

Court affirms its stance against tax affecting. The court noted that, even though both experts based their valuations on the DCF, they disagreed on major components of the analysis.

(i) *Cash-flow discounting.* The IRS's expert discounted the company's net EBITDA, whereas the estate's expert discounted its net free cash flows. "The parties have not distinguished between these two economic benefits against which to apply the DCF method," the court said. It preferred to derive the present value of the company's net cash flow but noted the lack of financial statements in evidence. Since the estate did not object to the revenue statements on which the IRS's expert relied, the court deemed these accurate but said it would develop its own operating income statements and growth rate (discussed below).

(ii) *Company projections.* Both experts prepared their own forecasts instead of relying on a multiyear forecast a bank had prepared in connection with the company's debt refinancing in 2004. This was the evidence available to the court.

The IRS's expert projected a 5.45% growth rate, based on the company's historical revenues. The estate's expert applied a 4.6% growth rate, based on industry rates and also the long-term growth rates of his public-company comparables. The court found the IRS's expert's revenue growth forecast was more persuasive, particularly since the estate's expert admitted his growth rate was significantly higher than the company's historical rates (0.6% to 1.1%). The IRS's expert also included revenues from the 2004 acquisition in his calculations, which were foreseeable at the valuation date. The court disregarded adjustments by the estate's expert for estimated newsprint costs, noting again that he failed to explain how he arrived at the costs, and it also disregarded his related operating margin projections and other expense adjustments. Modifying the IRS's expert's projected 39.5% operating margin slightly, the court concluded it was 36.4% of total revenue.

(iii) *Tax affecting.* Not surprisingly, the parties disagreed on the question of whether it was appropriate to tax affect the company's earnings under the DCF. The estate's expert applied a 39% income tax rate in calculating future cash flows and a 40% marginal tax rate to derive the discount rate. The IRS's expert chose to disregard shareholder-level taxes in projecting cash flow and in developing the applicable discount rate.

The court pointed out that the estate expert again failed to explain his reasons for his actions. "Absent an argument for tax affecting ... we decline to do so," the court said. It confirmed its ruling in *Gross v. Commissioner,* T.C. Memo. 199-254, that the "principal benefit enjoyed by S corporation shareholders is the reduction of their total tax burden."[134] Absent a reason for ignoring such benefit, the court declined to impose "an unjustified fictitious corporate tax rate burden on [the company's] future earnings."

(iv) *Cash-flow adjustments.* The IRS's expert based his capital expenditure assumption (2.8% of revenue) and working capital projections (-2.5% of revenue) on the company's historical financial data. The estate's expert developed his own projections, assuming capital expenditures would increase from 2.3% to 3.1% and projecting a fluctuating working capital. Because he provided no justification for his projections, the court disregarded them.

(v) *Rate of return.* Since both experts used the weighted average cost of capital (WACC) to determine a rate of return, the court adopted it but pointed out that "we do not set a general rule in doing so." It reminded the parties that "[w]e have previously held that WACC is an improper analytical tool to value a small closely held corporation with little possibility of going public."

The IRS's expert calculated a 10% WACC, assuming a 0% marginal tax rate, whereas the estate's expert calculated a 12.3% WACC using a 40% corporate tax rate. Based on its tax-affecting ruling, the court rejected the estate's approach and assumed a 0% tax rate in discounting the company's earnings.

The experts also disagreed on the cost of equity capital. The estate's expert used a CAPM formula to derive a 13.5% cost of equity; the IRS's expert used the build-up method, which yielded a 20% rate. Specifically, he started with an 11.7% equity risk premium from Ibbotson and added a 5.22% risk-free rate based on the *2004 Ibbotson Yearbook.* He next subtracted a 1% projected long-term growth rate to arrive at a minority capitalization

134 *Author's note:* Here, again, the Tax Court acknowledges that the benefit to an S corp shareholder is to *reduce its total tax burden.* However, the court has ignored *all tax burdens.* Any benefit to an S corp shareholder is the avoidance of dividend and capital gains taxes—the shareholder does not avoid taxes on corporate income.

rate, which he then converted to a market multiple; he then added a 20% control premium, a 4% company-specific risk premium, and a 2% S corp premium.

The court rejected the use of CAPM. But, while it approved of the IRS's expert's method, it took issue with his analysis. "We do not understand why [he] included [the] firm-specific risk premium as the final step … rather than considering it along with the risk-free rate and [ERP]," the court said. It modified his control premium from 20% to 30% to arrive at an 18% cost of capital.

With regard to the average cost of debt, the court once again criticized the estate's expert for failing to explain his 5% calculation and considered the IRS's expert's 6.6% rate reasonable. Finally, the court rejected the estate's expert's reliance on guideline company comparables for debt and equity ratios for the same reason it rejected the broad application of GCM, criticizing the estate's expert for his failure to provide an analysis and his "wavering stance." With reservations, the court adopted the constant 75% debt and 25% equity ratios the IRS's expert proposed while observing that "WACC is an improper discount rate tool for a company planning to pay down its debt." At the same time, the court made it clear that its finding here did not represent a general rule. It concluded the appropriate WACC was 10%.

(vi) *Adjustments to enterprise value.* In terms of long-term debt, both experts agreed on the categories of obligations but disagreed over the financial data on which to base their computations. The court adopted the figures from the IRS's expert because he based them on the more accurate June 2004 financial information. It noted that the estate's expert stated different debt amounts throughout the report, which made the numbers unreliable.

The court also said that the estate's expert "once again failed to explain" why he based his DCF working capital adjustment on a comparison to guideline comparables when he expressly considered the latter "not to be comparable" to the subject company and when he adequately had explained the need for the adjustment under the GCM but not the DCF. The court accorded little weight to "his seemingly contradictory positions" and disregarded his $900,000 working capital adjustment.

Importantly, in addition to tax affecting, the estate's expert also adjusted his DCF results by: (1) $12.8 million to account for "S shareholder tax savings" on the excess of future projected distributions over tax distributions; (2) $44.3 million to reflect the present value of the company's future deductible goodwill; and (3) $6.7 million for an extra marginal debt shield. Citing *Gross,* the expert asserted that these adjustments reflected the full economic value of the company's S corp status.

The court, however, found that, while the expert cited *Gross* correctly, his approach misconstrued the case. The court clarified that in *Gross* the taxpayer's expert accused the IRS's expert of failing to account for the "known payment" of taxes the shareholders of an S corp had to shoulder and argued in favor of applying the avoided C corp taxes as a hypothetical expense. But the court in *Gross* rejected the application of a hypothetical corporate tax, noting that the primary benefit to the S corp shareholders is "properly reflected through the imposition of a zero-percent corporate tax rate." Accordingly, the court in the present case found that *Gross* did not address the legitimacy of the other adjustments the estate's expert had made here, and it decided to disregard them.

Finally, both experts acknowledged they had to account for the company's stock option program, which was in effect on the valuation date, but disagreed on how best to capture its effect on the fair market value of the company. The estate's expert assumed the options all would vest and subtracted the expected, in-the-money proceeds, in the amount of $12.1 million, from the enterprise value. The IRS's expert calculated the per-unit fair market value of the options by dividing the option holders' equity by the total number of outstanding units as of the valuation date, ultimately concluding that the money received from the exercise of the options would simply increase the number of issued units rather than the company's cash flows. But since he did so "with no explanation," the court adopted the approach of the estate's expert albeit not his ultimate numbers.

(vii) *Determination of discounts.* Both experts agreed that it was appropriate in this case to consider minority and marketability discounts. The IRS's expert derived a minority discount based on his assumption that the inverse of a control premium equated to a minority interest discount. He relied on Mergerstat control premium data. Specifically, he found that the median premium paid in all industries was 34.4% in 2002 and 31.6% in 2003, and the premia paid in the newspaper sector ranged from 45.2% to 67.5%. He concluded that a 20% control premium was reasonable for the subject company, which equated to a 17% minority discount.

The estate's expert declined to apply a minority discount to his DCF because his analysis already accounted for the cash flows that accrued pro rata to all equity holders. He explained that consequently "the resulting firm value is on a minority interest basis and needs no further adjustment to reflect a minority interest value."

The court "generally" followed the IRS's expert's DCF approach, which derived equity value on a controlling basis, and, therefore, agreed that a minority discount was appropriate. But it found the IRS's expert "only vaguely supported" his selected control premium, which fell 10 percentage points below the industry median and 20 points below the premia in the newspaper sector. Absent a "more comprehensive explanation" from the expert, the court rejected his conclusion and decided that a 23% minority discount was appropriate.

There was little disagreement on the rate for the marketability discount. The IRS's expert assumed a 30% rate, whereas the estate's expert used a 31% rate. Both experts considered restricted stock studies, and the estate's expert also reviewed pre-IPO data at a slightly larger average discount. He also pointed out that the subject company's stock was "significantly more" restricted and was likely to incur longer holding periods.

"We have previously disregarded experts' conclusions as to marketability discounts for stock with holding periods of more than two years when based upon the above-referenced studies," the court noted. But, since in this case both experts' relied on the studies, the court accepted them as a "benchmark" and adopted the 31% discount.

Court's value approximates estate's original value. The court concluded that the decedent's 15% share in the company was worth $32.6 million on the valuation date. In effect, this value was close to the value the estate had stated in Form 706: $34.9 million.

Court issues subsequent revision. Note that, in a subsequent decision, *Estate of Gallagher v. Commissioner,* T.C. Memo 2011-244, the court issued a correction to its earlier computation and increased the value of the decedent's interest from $32.6 million to approximately $35.8 million.

■ *Delaware Open MRI Radiology Associates P.A. v. Kessler,* 808 A.2d 290, 2006 Del. Ch. LEXIS 84

Within the context of a squeeze-out merger, the Delaware Court of Chancery (Vice Chancellor Strine) performed a statutory appraisal to determine whether the merger price was fair to the minority stockholders and, if it was not, to calculate the extent of the underpayment. One significant component of the court's fair value determination was the vice chancellor's novel approach to quantify the value of the subject company as a going concern with an S corporation structure in order to award the minority shareholders their pro rata share of that value.

Background. A group of practicing radiologists formed a company in Delaware (Delaware Radiology) that owned centers at which patients received MRI scans. The impetus was to capture a larger part of the revenue stemming from providing radiology services. By owning the MRI centers and performing the diagnostic "reads" of the images, the radiologists would collect more of the total revenue generated from the treatment of patients. The first MRI center opened in 1998, and the second one opened in 1999. Under operating agreements, Delaware Radiology received 15% of the two centers' total revenues for doing the reading. Eventually, Delaware Radiology retained a third-party entity to handle the nonmedical aspects of the centers and paid it 1% of the centers' cash collection in management fees.

Various disputes among the doctors led to a split, turning the Delaware Radiology stockholders into two discrete blocks: the majority "Broder" group, which controlled 62.5% of the company, and the minority "Kessler" group, which owned the remaining 37.5%. Further competition among the shareholders resulted in the majority's setting up an acquisition company to "squeeze out" the minority group in a forced merger.

During 2003, the final year of joint ownership, the majority—Broder— group increased the reading fees for Center I to 17.5%. And it doubled the management firm's rate from 1% to 2%. It also used its control over Delaware Radiology to cut off the minority group from the profits flowing from the read work. The Broder group also actively pursued expansion throughout the state. It signed a lease for a third center and formed an operating company. Plans for a fourth center, which was owned by an entirely separate business, were also underway, with a lease ready for signature before the merger. There also was serious consideration of establishing a fifth center in the southern part of the state, although, at the time of the merger, the majority had not taken material steps toward realizing that plan. The operation of the additional centers followed the structure of the first two centers. The squeeze-out merger was effective on Jan. 20, 2004.

Also, in 2003, the Broder group hired a valuation analyst to calculate a price for the minority shares. The appraiser concluded it was approximately $16,000 per share. When the minority—Kessler—group dissented from the merger, Delaware Radiology proceeded to escalate the dispute and sued in the Delaware Court of Chancery to establish the fair value of the dissenters' interests. The Kessler group countersued, claiming breach of fiduciary duty, putting the burden on the Broder group to establish the entire fairness of the transaction.

The Chancery characterized the case as "one of our law's hybrid varietals: the combined appraisal and entire fairness action." The crux of the matter was whether the merger was financially fair. To answer that question, the court had to "determine the fair value of Delaware Radiology's shares on the merger date and award the Kessler Group a per-share amount consistent with their pro rata share of that value." The court cautioned that this exercise, requiring the valuation of "a small private company whose shares do not trade in a liquid and deep securities market, using a record shaped by adversaries whose objectives have little to do with reaching a reliable valuation, has, at best, the virtues of a good faith attempt at estimation."

Court distills three major valuation issues. The court found the Broder group's handling of the merger was not fair and proceeded to perform its own valuation. It determined that there were three key disputes over value: (1) the treatment of MRI "reading" and management fees; (2) the company's expansion plans at the time of the merger, from two to five MRI centers; and (3) the treatment of the company as an S corporation.

At trial, the Broder group offered testimony from the same expert who had performed the valuation setting the merger price. He used a discounted cash-flow analysis that: (1) accepted the reading and management fees as proper expenses of the company; (2) attributed "no value" to the company's known expansion plans; and (3) tax affected its earnings as if it were a C corp rather than an S corp. He applied "high" discount rates of 21.4% and 22.4% to the two MRI centers and arrived at a value of $6.8 million for Delaware Radiology, which translated to $17,039 per share.

The expert for the minority Kessler group also relied on a DCF analysis. But he: (1) reduced excessive management fees and treated the majority of reading fees as profit to the company rather than expenses to the MRI centers; (2) included an estimate for the proposed third and fourth centers but did not include an estimate for the most speculative fifth center; and (3) did not tax affect the company's earnings at all. He applied a lower discount rate to arrive at a value of $26.4 million for the company, or $66,074 per share.

The court reviewed each element as follows.

1. *Reading and management fees.* The court noted that, on this issue, "[b]oth sides took positions that did not have the ring of truth." When all the radiologists belonged to the same firm and shared equally in the MRI reading revenues, there was no unfairness in the amount Delaware Radiologists paid to the doctors. The problem began when the Broder group decided to cut the Kessler group out of the read work and transferred all of the reading fees to itself without making an adjustment for the prior above-market rate. The Kessler group claimed the amount improperly received by the Broder group was the difference between the lowest bidder price (what the court called "the bargain-basement option") and the amount the Broder group received (from 15% to as much as 17.5%).

The Chancery disagreed, finding that the proper offset should be the market rate of fees charged by comparable radiology groups. It looked to the "objective" Medicare reimbursement rate, which equated to a 13.7% fee. This was the most reliable evidence in the record, the court said, "premised on what is paid by one of the most important market payers in American health care." Accordingly, the court added the difference between the Medicare rate and the actual rate charged by the Broder group back to the revenue projections used to compute the fair value of the business.

As to the management fees, the court also found that the majority group had acted unfairly to the minority interests and halved the 2% fees.

2. *Company's expansion plans.* The court reminded the parties that, under Delaware law, "elements of future value, ... which are known or susceptible to proof as of the date of the merger and not the product of speculation, may be considered." Here it was "abundantly clear" that the company's "operative reality" included a strategy to expand MRI centers from two to four and that their value should figure into the fair value determination. The court observed that the more difficult question to answer was whether there was nonspeculative value for the fifth center.

The Chancery chastened the Broder group for insisting that not only was there no value attributable to the fifth center, but there was also none to the third and fourth centers. The majority's expert excluded the three projected centers entirely from his valuation report and testified that it was his "fundamental belief" that the projections were not relevant if the entities had not opened their doors at the time of the merger.

According to the court, "if that is true, [he] has a jarringly novel view of corporate finance, in which the value of McDonald's does not include the revenues it expects to make from the new franchises it will open." Consequently, the court included the full value of centers three and four, based on their projected earnings. And it included the value of the fifth center at one-third of the value of the fourth center. The court said this was to compensate the Kessler group for the "Broder Group's decision to usurp for itself the exclusive right to control the statewide network for itself."

3. *'Proper manner' to tax affect earnings of the S corp.* The Chancery noted that the Broder group's expert treated the company as if it were a C corp, making the "standard move" of applying a 40% corporate tax rate to its earnings. The court found this approach problematic, since there was absolutely no evidence that the small but highly profitable company would ever convert to a C corp. The court observed that the company's shareholders—all in premium tax brackets—placed a substantial value on the company's tax status as an S corp. The merger had deprived some of them of these benefits, and the majority's valuation approach "denied [them] the value they would have received as continuing S Corp stockholders," ensuring the merger price was lower than fair value.

On the other hand, the Kessler group's expert, relying on the "operative reality" of the S corp company, did not tax affect its earnings as a going concern. The court also rejected this approach. It overstated the value of the S corp at the stockholder level, as upon its sale an S corp receives no premium over a C corp from "a universe" of C corp buyers, and a market-based analysis using C corporation comparables is misleading.

According to the vice chancellor: "I am not trying to quantify the value at which [the company] would sell to a C corporation; I am trying to quantify [its] value ... as a going concern with an S corporation structure."

The challenge for the court was to "capture the precise advantage of the S corporation structure to the Kessler Group." This required using a method that quantifies the difference between the value that a stockholder of Delaware Radiology would receive in the company as a C corp and the value the shareholder would receive if the company was an S corp.

Court proposes a formula. For its analysis, the court "embraced" the leading Tax Court cases (*Gross*, *Heck*, and *Adams*), noting that they have "given life to the advantages of S corporation status by refusing to tax affect the ... earnings at all." But, said the vice chancellor:

> My difference with these prior decisions is at the level of implementation rather than at the level of principle. Certainly, in this context when minority stockholders have been forcibly denied the future benefits of S corporation status, they should receive compensation for those expected benefits and not an artificially discounted value that disregards the favorable tax treatment.... But the minority should not receive more than a fair S corporation valuation. Refusing to tax affect at all produces such a windfall.... The amount that should be the basis for an appraisal or entire fairness award is the amount that estimates the company's value to the [minority] as S corporation stockholders paying individual income taxes at the highest rates—an amount that is materially more ... than if the [company] were a C corporation.

To capture the value properly, the court estimated what an equivalent, hypothetical "predividend" S corporation tax rate would be, assuming annual earnings of $100 and highest marginal tax rates, according to Exhibit E-1.

Exhibit E-1. Equivalent, Hypothetical 'Predividend' S Corporation Tax Rate

	C Corp	S Corp	S Corp Valuation
Income before tax	$100	$100	$100
Corporate tax rate	40%	—	29.4%
Available earnings	$60	$100	$70.60
Dividend/personal income tax rate	15%	40%	15%
Total, post-tax distributions	$51	$60	$60

The court said that this calculation allowed it to treat the S corp shareholder as receiving the full benefit of untaxed dividends by equating its after-tax return to the after-tax dividend to a C corp shareholder.

The court decided to apply an effective tax rate of 29.4% to the earnings of Delaware Radiology to measure the fair value of the Kessler group's interest in the going-concern value.

Court performs its own DCF analysis. Having determined the major components of a DCF analysis, the court performed its own calculations. In so doing, it considered the two expert valuations in the case, using only those portions that were "credible and well-grounded in finance and fact."

It found the analysis the Kessler group's expert offered was more credible. He had approached his task "in a conservative and restrained manner that, although still reflecting a desire to advance his clients' objectives, reasonably took into account factors limiting the value" of the company.

The vice chancellor contrasted this approach with the attitude the Broder group's expert brought to his valuation:

> [His] testimony seemed more aggressively driven by his goal of reducing what the [majority] would be ordered to pay. Moreover, [he] was given his marching orders in his work before and after the merger that led him to undervalue [the company].... Put simply, this did not instill confidence in me.... [His] knowledge of the relevant facts regarding [the company] seemed unduly constrained by his clients, and his blinkered view of the business impaired his ability to reach a reasoned determination of value.

The court concluded the fair value of the company was $13.3 million, or $33,232 per share. The merger was unfair.

■ *Bernier v. Bernier*, 82 Mass. App. Ct. 81, 2012 Mass. App. LEXIS 211

In a multilayered divorce case involving the valuation of two S corporations, the Massachusetts Supreme Court ordered the trial court to use the tax-affecting approach the Delaware Court of Chancery had developed in the *Kessler* case. However, uncertainty over the applicable dividend tax rate created further disagreement among the parties as to the correct approach. On first remand, the trial court rejected both parties' valuations and decided to use the very tax-affecting rate the *Kessler* court used—29.4%—but its decision prompted both parties to appeal. The Appeals Court of Massachusetts found the trial court's approach failed "to capture the tax benefit to the buyer of S corporation shares of receiving taxable cash dividends that were not already taxed at the corporate level." It remanded, again.

History of the case. During their marriage, the husband and the wife operated two supermarkets that were owned by two S corporations that the parties owned in equal measure. The business was a financial success. At the initial divorce trial in 2002, the parties' principal area of contention was the value of the supermarkets. Both parties retained valuation experts who agreed on a valuation date (Dec. 31, 2000) and on applying the income approach. But the experts disagreed over tax affecting and the use of discounts to arrive at the business's fair market value.

In particular, the husband's expert tax affected the S corps as if they were C corporations, applying the then-average corporate rate of 35% as well as key person and lack of marketability discounts to reach a fair market value of $7.85 million. He reasoned that a potential buyer of an S corp would consider the tax consequences of the purchase when determining a rate of return. The wife's expert neither tax affected nor applied discounts and valued the stores at nearly $16.4 million. He maintained that an S corp did not pay taxes at the corporate level and the parties did not contemplate a sale of the business. The trial court found the valuation of the wife's expert "unreliable" and for the most part adopted the valuation the husband's expert proposed, including the expert's tax-affecting method and discounts.

The wife appealed to the Supreme Judicial Court, which concluded that the trial court had erred by adopting the husband's tax-affecting approach. The state's high court said that applying a C corp's rate of taxation to an S corp "severely undervalues the fair market value of the S corporation by ignoring the tax benefits of the S corporation structure and failing to compensate the seller for the loss of those benefits." This approach was particularly inappropriate under the facts of the case. For example, it was clear that the supermarkets would continue to operate as S corps after the parties' divorce and that the business would be owned by the present shareholders and, as in the past, would continue to make cash distributions.

But the state Supreme Court also noted that the failure to tax affect an S corp at all would artificially inflate the company's value by overstating the retaining shareholders' expected rate of return. Considering the "scant case law" and other authority on the subject, the high court sent the case back to the trial court, directing it to adopt the metric employed in *Delaware Open MRI Radiology Associates. v. Kessler*, 898 A.2d 290 (Del. Ch. 2006).

According to the Massachusetts Supreme Court, in the *Kessler* case, the Delaware Court of Chancery tried "to capture the tax benefit to the buyer of S corporation shares (the majority shareholders) of receiving cash dividends that are not subject to dividend taxes." To this end, the Chancery assumed a dividend rate of 15% and a personal income tax rate of 40% to impute a "predividend" rate of 29.4%. It noted that applying this rate to the earnings of the pass-through entity measures "with the greatest practicable precision" the fair value of the going concern.

The Massachusetts high court allowed that, since *Kessler* came after the trial court's initial ruling, the latter did not have the benefit of its reasoning. But it added that the lower court should have risen above the "all-or-nothing" approach of the parties' experts and given greater consideration to the facts of the case. Remanding, the Supreme Court directed the trial court "to employ the tax affecting approach adopted in *Kessler*."

Confusion over interpreting Supreme Court's ruling. On remand, the high court's directive to use the "*Kessler* metric" or the "*Kessler* approach" created uncertainty and disagreement between the parties, in large part due to a change in federal income tax treatment of corporate dividends. In *Kessler*, the valuation date was January 2004, when the applicable dividend tax rate was 15%, but in 2000—the valuation date in this case—the rate was 40%. Since the Massachusetts Supreme Court did not address the rate change, the trial court and the parties had no guidance on what specific rates the high court wanted them to use in applying the "*Kessler* metric."

The wife's new expert, a credentialed business appraiser, testified that he used the formula set forth in *Kessler* but input the dividend rate that was applicable in 2000. It was 40%. Because the personal income tax rate at the stipulated valuation date was also 40%, the effect was a 0% tax-affecting rate. Based on the tax-affecting rate of zero, the wife's expert concluded the supermarkets had a combined value of $14 million as of 2000.

In contrast, the husband retained a CPA who had never conducted a business valuation but whom the trial court qualified as a tax expert. Since an S corporation's earnings are taxable to the shareholders at state and federal ordinary income tax rates, this expert applied a 5.85% Massachusetts rate and a 39.6% federal rate, as well as a state S corp tax at the entity level, which was in effect in 2000. The trial court found he tax affected at approximately 46% combined rate to conclude that the supermarkets were worth approximately $9.3 million.

The trial court discredited both approaches. It said that using a 0% tax-affecting rate, as the wife's expert did, ignored the "clear mandate" of the Supreme Court to do something because not to tax affect "was unfair." At the same time, the valuation by the husband's expert ignored the implicit finding in *Bernier I* that any tax-affecting rate above 35% would undervalue the businesses. According to the court, to apply a 46% rate, which substantially exceeded the 35% rate the husband originally proposed for his valuation, "would lead to an even more significant undervaluation of the supermarkets." Having rejected both experts' opinions, it strictly applied the 29.4% rate from the *Kessler* case. It reasoned that this was the only rate it could use in light of the Supreme Judicial Court's reliance on *Kessler*. The trial court found the combined value of the supermarkets was approximately $11 million.

Both parties claimed error in the trial court's valuation and appealed the decision to the state's appeals court.

Appeals court refutes trial court's application of *Kessler* metric. The wife argued the trial court was under order to apply strictly the *Kessler* method, not simply the rate the *Kessler* court used based on the facts before the Delaware Chancery. Then the valuation date was 2004, not 2000, as in the present case. Although the husband conceded that applying the applicable 2000 rates would net a tax affecting of zero, he argued that the decisions in *Bernier I* as well as *Kessler* and the Massachusetts Supreme Court's own decision in *Adams v. Adams*, 459 Mass 361 (2011), stood for the proposition that "subchapter S corporation earnings must be tax affected to avoid an inequitable result in the valuation process." The "accident of timing" as far as the tax rates were concerned should not control the outcome of the case. He suggested that, instead of applying the *Kessler* metric strictly on the "basis of pure mathematics," the more equitable solution would be to use the federal and state tax rates in effect in 2000—as his expert had done.

The Massachusetts Court of Appeals decided the wife presented a more "cogent position" than either the trial court or the husband. The Supreme Court "adopted generally the metric employed by the *Kessler* court," and it ordered the trial court on remand to apply the tax-affecting approach of *Kessler*. Only the wife's expert offered a valuation consistent with the mandate. According to the appeals court, "application of the *Kessler* metric, even as it results … in a zero percent tax affecting rate, does not necessarily lead to an inequitable result." The appeals court added:

> There is a distinction … between failing to tax affect at all the earnings of the supermarkets because an S corporation does not pay federal taxes at the entity level (a basis for the approach taken by the wife's expert … in *Bernier I*), and utilizing a zero percent tax affecting rate arrived at through application of "all applicable rates," as the [Supreme Judicial Court] ordered.

The *Kessler* approach tries to capture the tax benefit to the buyer of S corporation shares of receiving taxable cash dividends that were not already taxed at the corporate level and does so by calculating "the effect of taxes on the buyers and the sellers." The appeals court further observed that the metric prompts a trial judge to ask: "If the S corporation at issue were a C corporation, at what hypothetical tax rate could it be taxed and still leave to shareholders the same amount in their pockets as they would have if they held shares in an S corporation?"[135] Because the applicable dividend tax rate in 2000 was 40%, a tax-affecting rate of zero was "necessary to achieve that result."[136]

While the appeals court expressly recognized that the trial judge sought to reach what she viewed as an equitable result in a difficult and complex case, it found that her ultimate value determination, based on a 29.4% tax-affecting rate, was indefensible. The 29.4% tax rate bore no relationship to, and was contrary to, the parties' stipulated valuation date of Dec. 31, 2000.

The court also pointed out that, even if it were to accept the husband's argument in favor of a general application of the *Kessler* approach, rather than a "literal" application, he failed to present evidence that his expert's methodology constituted an accepted form of tax affecting for valuing an S corporation. The court emphasized that the husband's expert was qualified only in tax matters. The husband did not present a business valuation expert who could testify specifically to tax affecting as part of a traditional and commonly accepted appraisal.

The appeals court also found the husband's reliance on the *Adams* case misplaced. "[W]e fail to discern anything in that case that would cause us to reach a different result." Accordingly, the appeals court remanded the case—once again—to the trial court for a valuation of the parties' S corporations consistent with its opinion as well as *Bernier I*. In so doing, it noted that the trial court could also order additional evidentiary hearings as necessary to reach a proper result.

■ *Estate of Giustina v. Commissioner*, 2014 U.S. App. LEXIS 22961 (Dec. 5, 2014)

In a significant ruling, the 9th Circuit faulted the U.S. Tax Court for several technical missteps in arriving at its valuation of the decedent's minority interest in a limited

135 *Author's note:* The relevant question is: "If the S corporation at issue were a public C corporation ..." This is because the purpose of any adjustment is to account for any mismatch in the *public-market return* used to value the S corp.

136 *Author's note:* The court used the current, statutory rate to make its adjustment. As this guide has discussed extensively, the current statutory rate overstates the magnitude of any adjustment needed. This is because we are adjusting for a mismatch between the cost of capital and the cash flow. The cost of capital has embedded in it tax effects that have occurred over the long-horizon over which the return was developed.

partnership holding considerable timber assets. However, the appeals court upheld the Tax Court's decision on tax affecting, noting this was an unsettled area of law.

Background. The decedent owned a minority interest in a family-owned limited partnership (LP) that was in operation for 15 years and held large tracts of local timberland. The Internal Revenue Service (IRS) assessed a deficiency of $12.66 million, which was nearly equal to the value the estate stated in its estate tax filing, and an accuracy-related penalty. The estate petitioned the U.S. Tax Court for a review. At trial, the parties' positions had come closer together because the estate's new appraiser proposed a slightly higher value and the IRS's expert a slightly lower value.

The Tax Court accepted only two methods to value the LP interest in this case: discounted cash flow (DCF) and net asset value (NAV). The former accounted for how much the partnership could be expected to earn if it continued timberland operations, and the latter valued the assets as if liquidated. The experts agreed the partnership's timber assets were worth $143 million, allowing for a 40% discount related to expected delays in selling the large tracts. However, they weighted the values from the two approaches differently and disagreed on assumptions inherent in the cash-flow approach.

As for the DCF, the court not only rejected the IRS's expert's analysis, but also adjusted components of the estate's expert's valuation. For one, it lowered the latter's 3.5% company-specific risk premium, noting that, even though the partnership's assets lacked diversity and geographic dispersion, investors could minimize this unique risk by diversifying the portfolio of assets. Therefore, a 1.75% premium was adequate. The court also found that, pursuant to *Gross v. Commissioner*, the estate's expert improperly tax affected his annual cash-flow values by 25%. And the court reduced the expert's proposed 35% discount for lack of marketability to 25% in accordance with the rate the IRS's expert applied.

The court gave a 75% weighting to the DCF-derived value, which, it found, reflected the probability that the partnership would continue. But it also noted that an asset sale would reap considerably more than the current cash flow generated. The court recognized that an acquirer of the decedent's interest could only force the sale of the partnership by creating a two-thirds majority voting block with other members and that it was uncertain how many partners would favor an asset sale. But it said there was authority that allowed for some degree of speculation about the future composition of management in valuation and consequently assigned a 25% weight to the result from the NAV. It concluded the decedent's interest was worth $27.45 million.

Ninth Circuit rejects use of NAV. In its appeal to the 9th Circuit Court of Appeals, the estate claimed there were multiple errors in the Tax Court's valuation, which stated a value that was close to $15 million higher than the estate's value appearing in Form 706.

The 9th Circuit sided with the estate on most points.

1. *NAV weight.* According to the appeals court, the Tax Court's finding that there was a 25% likelihood of liquidation of the partnership conflicted with the evidence in the record. This was a longtime partnership, and "no limited partner ever asked or ever discussed the sale of an interest," said the 9th Circuit. For liquidation to occur, one had to assume that a hypothetical buyer would: (1) "somehow" obtain admission as a limited partner from the general partners to dissolve the partnership; (2) seek to dissolve the partnership or get rid of the general partners who just approved the buyer's admission to the partnership; and (3) succeed in persuading at least two other limited partners to go along with the buyer's plan.

Alternatively, and just as unlikely, the appeals court said, one had to assume that the existing limited partners who owned two-thirds of the partnership would suddenly seek dissolution.

According to the 9th Circuit, the Tax Court created "imaginary scenarios" as to the potential buyer and the buyer's willingness to wait, without receiving a return on the investment, as well as what the buyer would be able to arrange with the existing partners. For this reason alone, the 9th Circuit remanded for a revaluation based on the partnership's value as a going concern.

2. *Company-specific risk.* In addition, the Court of Appeals found error in the Tax Court's halving the estate's expert's proposed company-specific risk premium. Although diversification of assets was an accepted way to reduce company-specific risk, the Tax Court did not seem to take into account how much wealth a potential buyer would need to affect diversification.

Ninth Circuit declines to upend tax-affecting finding. On several points, the 9th Circuit disagreed with the estate. As for tax affecting, the Court of Appeals pointed out that the estate admitted that "tax-affecting is … an unsettled matter of law." Therefore, the 9th Circuit found it was not clear that the Tax Court erred in using a pretax rather than a post-tax method.

As for the DLOM rate, the estate's expert proffered a 35% rate but at trial allowed that discounts typically range between 25% and 35%. Accordingly, the Tax Court's 25% DLOM was not clear error.

For all of these reasons, the 9th Circuit remanded for recalculation of the valuation.

■ *Hamelink v. Hamelink,* 2014 Minn. App. Unpub. LEXIS 1175 (Dec. 30, 2013), *further review denied,* 2014 Minn. LEXIS 149 (Feb. 26, 2014)

Since *Bernier v. Bernier,* courts have been relatively silent on the issue of how to account for an S corporation owner's personal taxes on company profits in the context of divorce. A Minnesota appeals court decision is noteworthy precisely because the court discussed the effect of foundational cases such as *Gross, Kessler,* and *Bernier* on business valuation for marital distribution purposes. But the court provided no clear answer to the question of whether to tax affect. Instead, the decision reflects a court that is at once receptive and noncommittal to adopting the technique.

Experts disagree over tax affecting. The husband founded a successful company that designed and manufactured custom burner equipment for fireplaces, grills, furnaces, and commercial ovens. The company was organized as an S corporation, and he was the sole owner.

At divorce, both spouses offered expert testimony as to the value of the business. The experts disagreed on the valuation methodology and, by extension, on the fair market value of the company.

The central valuation issue was whether to tax affect. As the court defined it:

> Tax affecting is the technique of valuing S corporations by considering the effect of a hypothetical buyer's personal tax liability on estimated earnings. This technique is implemented by calculating and applying a hypothetical tax rate, which effectively lowers estimated future earnings and the fair market value derived from such earnings.

Both experts used an income approach. The husband's expert computed the fair market value of the company by using the single-period capitalization method while tax affecting estimated future earnings. By his account, the business was worth nearly $2.3 million.

The wife's expert performed a discounted cash flow analysis and, without tax affecting, arrived at a value of $6.5 million. He explained that he based his decision not to tax affect primarily on *Gross v.* Commissioner, T.C. Memo 1999-254, *aff'd,* 272 F.3d 333 (6th Cir. 2001). In *Gross,* the Tax Court rejected tax affecting, noting: "We believe the principal benefit that shareholders expect from an S corporation election is a reduction in the total tax burden imposed on the enterprise ... and we see no reason why that savings ought to be ignored as a matter of course in valuing the S corporation."[137]

---

137 *Authors' note:* The tax court acknowledges that it is a *reduction in the total tax burden* that the shareholders expect in an S corporation. The court goes on, however, not to reflect a reduction in the tax burden, but rather,

In addition, the expert relied on a Minnesota district court decision (slip opinion) in which the trial court rejected tax affecting in the context of a forced buyout. *See Doerr v. Arundel,* No. EM 97-013502 (Minn. Dist. Ct. Oct. 1, 1999). The court in *Doerr* explained its position by focusing on the hypothetical seller's willingness to sell, noting that it was much more likely that the hypothetical sale would be to another S corp. "With this in mind, it only makes sense for the court to conclude that it is unlikely that a willing seller would choose to sell the business to a C corporation instead of an S corporation, for less than the business is worth to the seller."

In the instant case, the trial court adopted the approach the wife's expert proposed but adjusted some of the components underlying the DCF analysis to arrive at a value of $3.7 million. (According to the appellate opinion, the adjustments were of no consequence to the appeal.)

Husband says 'national law' requires tax affecting in divorce cases. The husband appealed the decision at the Minnesota Court of Appeals. He argued that the district court erred in refusing to use the after-tax value for its valuation of the company and, therefore, overvalued the company by approximately $700,000.

He contended that the cases the wife's expert cited in support of his decision not to tax affect were not divorce cases. The husband went further, claiming that "[i]n the context of divorce, national case law makes clear that in order to arrive at an accurate value, the [c]ourt must tax affect the business." Specifically, he advocated for the hybrid tax-affecting approach that the Delaware Court of Chancery developed in *Delaware Open MRI Radiology Associates P.A. v. Kessler* and that the Massachusetts Supreme Court ordered the lower case to apply in the marriage dissolution context in *Bernier.*

In *Kessler,* the issue was "whether the minority stockholders of [an S corporation] received fair value in a squeeze-out merger with an acquisition vehicle of the majority shareholders." The Chancery refused both experts' approaches: (1) to tax affect at a hypothetical full corporate rate of 40%; or (2) not to tax affect at all. Instead, it tried to "quantify the actual benefits of the S corporation status" by first calculating a cash flow with no corporate taxes and a 40% personal tax rate and then using the cash flow and a 15% personal dividend tax rate to arrive at a 29.4% hypothetical corporate rate.

to *eliminate the entire tax burden* of the S corporation. The benefit of a reduction in the total tax burden would not be the total elimination of it, but rather, an adjustment for the difference in the tax burden of a public C corporation versus the S corporation. This distinction has the effect of significantly overvaluing the S corporation.

In *Bernier v. Bernier*, a divorce case centering on the valuation of the parties' supermarket business, the Massachusetts Supreme Court decided that the *Kessler* hybrid approach was a "fairer mechanism for accounting for the tax consequences of the transfer of ownership of the supermarkets from one spouse to the other."

Appeals court gives nod to tax affecting. At the outset of its review, the appeals court in the instant case noted that the district court's opinion was based on admissible expert testimony and the valuation methodology had support in the record. Accordingly, the appeals court was unable to say with "definite and firm conviction that the district court's valuation fell outside a reasonable range of figure."

However, the Court of Appeals acknowledged that no Minnesota appellate court had decided the tax affecting issue in the divorce context, and it allowed that the husband's position in favor of tax affecting had "some weight," even though he "overstates the level of support" for it.

The court pointed out that *Kessler* also was not a divorce case but a combined appraisal and fairness action. Nevertheless, together, *Kessler* and *Bernier* offered support for the decision by the husband's expert not to tax affect.

But the Court of Appeals made it clear that this determination was not the end of the analysis. As an error-correcting court, it had to decide whether the district court's refusal to tax affect was an abuse of discretion. It found that it was not. For one, the husband's expert admitted, "The issue of tax affecting is an open debate." The court also found that the difference between divorce and nondivorce cases, of which the husband made much, was "superficial" and of no consequence to the heart of the issue:[138] how to determine the value at which a business would change hands between a hypothetical willing buyer and a hypothetical willing seller.

The husband's argument that ignoring the personal taxes of an S corp owner would result in overvaluation also had no traction with the appeals court. Pointing to valuation literature, the court noted that, when it came to the valuation of C corporations, the courts, the IRS, and the valuation profession in general for decades have accepted the practice of ignoring the effect of personal tax liability. See Keith F. Sellers and Nancy J. Fannon, *Valuation of Pass-Through Entities: Looking at the Bigger Picture* 2 (2011).

138 *Authors' note:* In the Dallas case, the tax court made a distinction between fair market value and fair value. Here, the Minnesota Supreme Court discusses the distinction between divorce and nondivorce cases. However, regardless of the standard of value, the analyst is using a return from the public market to value the private company. That return has tax effects embedded in it that don't match the pass-through entity. It is this mismatch analysts adjust for, regardless of the standard of value.

Therefore, the appeals court continued, "we do not find it unreasonable to employ the same practice for the valuation of S corporations in a hypothetical transaction." Finally, it stated: "Whether to do so is for the experts to explain, the parties to prove, and the district court to decide."[139]

The appeals court also was not receptive to the husband's warning, at oral argument, that a failure to adopt a pro-tax-affecting stance meant the wife's expert would continue to testify in upcoming divorce cases and "no district court would ever find tax affecting to be appropriate." It cautioned litigants not to read its decision in the instant case to stand for the proposition that "tax affecting should never be considered."

In the same vein, the Court of Appeals rejected the wife's claim that Tax Court case law "indicat[ed] that hypothetical tax burdens are not a basis for manipulating a company's value." The appeals court said it did not read the decision in *Gross* to set forth this bright-line rule against tax affecting. The court went further. "*Gross* actually advocated for tax affecting under the right circumstances." For this proposition, the appeals court cited with emphasis the statement in *Gross*: "If ... the discount rate is assumed to be an after-shareholder-tax rate of return, then the cash-flow should be reduced ('tax affected') to an after-shareholder-tax amount."[140] According to the appeals court, *Gross* was "really only concerned with matching the tax characteristics of the discount rate and cash flow, which is sound economic principle."

Should a trial court confront the question of whether to tax affect in the future, it had discretion to consider *Gross, Kessler,* and *Bernier* in reaching a decision, the Court of Appeals said, and affirmed the trial court's valuation.

■ *Bank of America, N.A. v. Veluchamy (In re Veluchamy),* 2014 Bankr. LEXIS 5106 (Dec. 18, 2014)

A complex bankruptcy decision adjudicating over 20 claims of fraudulent transfers includes an informative discussion on tax affecting by reputed valuation experts who were charged with calculating the value of stock in one of the defendants' S corporations. The court agreed with the defendant expert's proposition that an accurate valuation had to consider the taxation of the shareholders on the company's earnings but disapproved of the way in which the expert translated this principle into practice when calculating the company's cash flow.

139 *Authors' note:* As discussed throughout this guide, *no court has yet been presented evidence* as to the effect of taxes on value.

140 *Authors' note:* It is precisely this issue that this guide has addressed.

Background. The defendants, husband and wife, established a number of direct-mailing and marketing operations. When those businesses proved a success, they invested in banking institutions but foundered when the government began to investigate the institutions' loan practices and financial conditions. To keep the banks afloat, the defendants borrowed tens of millions of dollars from a predecessor of Bank of America (BofA), the plaintiff.

Before the defendants defaulted on their loans, they reported a net worth of nearly $500 million. But when BoA took measures to collect the outstanding loans, the defendants conceived and carried out a scheme to dispose of almost all of their major assets and thus place them out of reach of creditors. The plan included selling stock and real estate in the U.S. and India at discounted prices to their two children and other family members and giving them the remaining cash and other assets, such as jewelry. When BoA was poised to go to trial to collect on judgments totaling over $47 million, the defendants filed for Chapter 7 bankruptcy and caused their businesses to file for Chapter 11 bankruptcy.

In the Chapter 7 case, BoA came to represent the estate because its interests aligned with those of the trustee and other creditors. The plaintiff presented 23 claims for fraudulent transfers. The Bankruptcy Court found the plaintiff "amply" proved liability and fashioned a remedy for each of the counts based on expert testimony. One count in particular raised important issues for valuators.

The dispute centered on the defendants' sales of stock in a holding company, operating as an S corp, which, in turn, owned seven profitable direct marketing companies.

Before the contested stock sales, the defendants owned a 70% interest in the company and a right to most of its income. Their two children owned the remainder of the stock, 15% each. Once BoA filed suit against the defendants, the latter orchestrated two transfers to sell a controlling interest in the company to their two children for less than fair value by having the company issue new shares. The result was a dilution of the defendants' interest from 70% to 19.8% in voting stock and from 70% to 52.0% in nonvoting stock. Transferring control of the company to the children meant that any creditor who seized the defendants' stock would be unable to control the company and its subsidiaries.

The court found the sales represented a fraudulent transfer.

Court favors income approach for valuing company. In terms of remedy, since the estate wanted to obtain a cash award rather than the children's interest in the proceeds of the subject company's bankruptcy sale, it had the burden of establishing the value of the shares at the time of the transfers. The estate's expert used both a market and an income approach.

Market approach. To compute the subject company's value, he selected a number of publicly traded companies that he said were similar to the subject company and applied average sales and earnings multiples from the chosen group to the subject's sales and earnings. (The opinion does not provide specifics.)

The defendants' expert maintained that the selection included some companies that were much larger than the subject and others that were "penny stock" companies whose precarious financial situation put them at risk of being delisted from the exchanges on which their stock traded. He also questioned the way in which the estate's expert had derived multiples from the selected set's financial data.

According to the court, these criticisms did not invalidate the market approach, but they were important enough to make the income approach the more persuasive valuation method. It decided the modifications (see below) the estate expert's analysis provided "a reasonable value" of the value of the stock.

Income approach. Under the income approach, the estate's expert performed a capitalization of net cash flow analysis. The defendants' expert objected to elements of the normalized cash flow analysis and the determination of the capitalization rate.

One point of contention centered on estimating future capital expenditures. Because the estate's expert lacked access to the company's cash flow statements, he estimated future capital expenditures that would lower normalized cash flow. In so doing, he added a smaller amount of depreciation in calculating the normalized cash flow for the relevant year than the company had deducted from income in the past.

The defendants' expert claimed the estate expert's calculation of the expenditures was incorrect. Capital expenditures must equal depreciation costs, he claimed; otherwise, "the assets of [the] company would disappear within five years because of lack of replenishment and replacement."

The court found this claim was without basis. "Fully depreciated property may continue to be used or it may be discarded either with no need for replacement or with the replacement incurring a lower cost." It observed that the estate's expert used an amount that was smaller than the historical deduction, "presumably because the deduction available to [the company] would be declining." According to the court, the amount of capital expenditures was independent of the depreciation costs.

A second disagreement concerned the estate's expert inclusion of the defendants' compensation in the annual cash flow. He explained he did this because the defendants did not provide remunerative services but simply took equity distribution in the form of compensation.

The defendants' expert said that adding the compensation to the cash flow was error since only a controlling shareholder would be able to prevent the defendants from withdrawing excessive personal payments from the company.

The court sided with the estate's expert. It noted that the stock transfers conveyed control to the children, who together had control of the business. Under applicable law, there was an assumption that siblings likely would work together to control a business. Also, the company had management that was separate from the defendants. The court determined that a third party acquiring the children's interests would be able to stop the defendants from withdrawing "inappropriate" compensation. Therefore, it was appropriate to increase the amount of income for the company by the amount of the compensation the defendants had withdrawn.

Court adopts rationale for tax affecting, if not methodology. The estate expert's decision not to tax affect the company's income represented another area of disagreement. He explained that whether and how to account for the taxation applicable to S corporations was a matter of debate in the valuation community. Moreover, he said, multiple decisions from the U.S. Tax Court have held that it is inappropriate to reduce the value of an S corp to capture the tax effects on S corp owners.

The defendants' expert argued that it was a mistake not to tax affect. The value of the subject company should be reduced by the tax that a theoretical purchaser of its shares would have to pay on its income. He pointed out that, even though the owner of an S corporation's stock avoids the double taxation imposed on the owner of an ordinary C corporation, there was still taxation of the individual owner on the income of the S corporation. According to him, the correct way to include this tax effect in the valuation of an S corp was to charge the corporation's income with taxes at a rate reduced by its owners' tax savings.[141]

In his valuation, the defendants' expert adjusted the company's income by reducing "Income Before Taxes" by 38%. The rate was based on 35% and 3% federal and state

141 *Authors' note:* This method is effectively the method adopted by the Delaware Chancery Court in *Delaware Open MRI*, discussed in this appendix. However, the expert failed to carry the method out as he described it (deducting a corporate tax burden but failing to adjust it for the benefit of the avoided dividend and capital gains tax).

ordinary income tax rates, respectively.

The court found the defendant expert's reasoning was persuasive, but he did not execute the approach he proposed. Therefore, the court did not adopt his calculation. The Bankruptcy Court noted: "Purchasers of S corporations would in fact experience a reduction in the value of the corporations' earnings because of the need to pay personal income taxes on those earnings, and recognizing that tax effect in valuing S corporations is appropriate."

At the same time, it said the defendant expert's calculation simply reduced the company's income by the marginal tax rate of individual owners, which was higher than the rate corporations would pay. Moreover, the expert failed to reflect the savings flowing from the elimination of the double taxation.

Ultimately, rather than correct the defendant expert's calculation to align with the approach—correct—which he advocated, the Bankruptcy Court decided to choose the midpoint between the defendant expert's tax-affected net cash flow ($7.3 million) and the estate expert's non-tax-affected cash flow ($8.5 million). According to court, $7.9 million was the amount to be used in the estate expert's income-based valuation.

Court adjusts capitalization rate. The court also found that the defendants' expert raised several valid concerns about the competing expert's calculation of the discount rate. The first related to the estate expert's use of a company-specific risk premium. The defendants' expert explained the valuation profession disfavored its use and proposed the application of an approximately 2.9% industry risk adjustment (the text provides conflicting rates) based on Ibbotson. The court agreed.

The experts also discussed the appropriateness of an additional small-firm risk premium. The defendants' expert suggested applying a discount at a rate of 5.9%, whereas the estate's expert noted that studies showed that purchasers did not currently apply small-firm risk premiums. The court rejected an all-or-nothing approach and chose to apply a 2.95% rate.

The estate's expert provided a high rate and a low rate for the equity risk premium—4.36% and 5.00%—based on "two reliable sources." The defendants' expert had no objections, but the court said the midpoint rate—4.68%—"is the best reflection of the evidence."

Factoring in these changes, the court concluded the appropriate capitalization rate was 11.66%. When it applied this rate to the $7.9 million annualized cash flow, it arrived at a value of nearly $68 million at the relevant time.

Court sides with estate's expert on DLOM. Both experts agreed that the valuation should include a discount for lack of marketability to recognize the difficulty a seller would experience in finding willing buyers. They disagreed over the applicable rate. The defendants' expert proposed a 35% rate. He claimed this rate adequately accounted for the increased difficulty of selling an interest in a business controlled by others. The estate's expert used a 15% rate.

The court credited the estate's expert, noting that the defendants' children received a controlling interest by way of the two fraudulent stock sales.

The Bankruptcy Court next considered the percentage of outstanding stock the children received in the two transfers to calculate the children's individual liability. It found that they each were liable to the estate for $1.37 million for the initial stock transfer and $7.9 million for the second transfer. In total, under this one count for fraudulent transfer alone, each child was liable for nearly $9.3 million.

Appendix F. Bibliography

Ashok B. Abbott, "The Role of Liquidity in Asset Pricing," www. bvlibrary.com/Search. aspx?scp=BVResearchandscq=NYSE.

Ashok B. Abbott, "Untangling the Web of Discounts: Marketability, Liquidity, and Control Issues in Valuation: An Empirical Estimation of Holding Period for Listed Securities," University of San Diego School of Law Business Valuation Conference: Summit on Discount for Lack of Marketability, San Diego, Sept. 18, 2008, www.bvresources.com.

Franklin Allen and Roni Michaely, "Payout Policy," Chapter 7 of G.M. Constantinides, M. Harris, and R. M. Stulz, *Guide of the Economics of Finance,* 2003, Ed. 1, Vol. 1, Elsevier.

Gene Amromin, Paul Harrison, and Steven Sharpe, "How Did the 2003 Dividend Tax Cut Affect Stock Prices?" *Finance and Economics Discussion,* 2005, Paper No. 2005-61.

Aviva Aron-Dine, "Study Finds Dividend Tax Cut Failed to Boost Stock Prices," *Center on Budget and Policy Priorities,* Dec. 12, 2005.

Gerald Auten, "Capital Gains Taxation," Department of the Treasury, in Joseph J. Cordes, Robert D. Ebel, and Jane G. Gravelle, eds., *The Encyclopedia of Taxation and Tax Policy,* 1999, Urban Institute Press.

Benjamin C. Ayers, C. Bryan Cloyd, and John R. Robinson, "The Effect of Shareholder-Level Dividend Taxes on Stock Prices: Evidence From the Revenue Reconciliation Act of 1993," *The Accounting Review,* October 2002, Vol. 77, No. 4.

Jennifer L. Blouin, "A Discussion of Tax-Based Dividend Clienteles: Evidence From Tax Law Changes," *Journal of the American Taxation Association* Conference, Feb. 22, 2008.

Jennifer L. Blouin, Jana Smith Raedy, and Douglas A. Shackelford, "Did Dividends Increase Immediately After the 2003 Reduction in Tax Rates?" *National Bureau of Economic Research*, February 2004, Working Paper No. 10301, www.nber.org/papers/w10301.

Jennifer L. Blouin, Jana Smith Raedy, and Douglas A. Shackelford, "The Initial Impact of the 2003 Reduction in the Dividend Tax Rate," *National Bureau of Economic Research* (University of Pennsylvania, University of North Carolina, and NBER; www.nber.org), October 2004.

Jennifer L. Blouin, Jana Smith Raedy, and Douglas A. Shackelford, "Did Firms Substitute Dividends for Share Repurchases After the 2003 Reductions in Shareholder Tax Rates?" Working Paper 13601, *NBER Working Paper Series*, www.nber.org/papers/w13601.

Marshall E. Blume, Donald B. Keim, Howard Butcher, III, and John B. Neff, "The Changing Preferences of Institutional Investors for Common Stocks," March 11, 2014.

William T. Bogart and William M. Gentry, "Capital Gains Taxation and Realizations: Evidence From Interstate Comparisons," NBER Working Paper No. W42254, last revised Jan. 7, 2002.

Paul J. Bolster and Vahan Janjigian, "Dividend Policy and Valuation Effects of the Tax Reform Act of 1986," *National Tax Journal*, December 1991, Vol. 44, No. 4.

Carolyn Kay Brancato and Stephan Rabimov, "U.S. Institutional Investors Boost Control of U.S. Equity Markets," *The 2005 Institutional Investment Report: U.S. and International Trends*, October 2005.

Eugene F. Brigham and Joel F. Houston, Fundamentals of Financial Management, 8th ed., South-Western (Division of Thomson Learning), 1998.

Raj Chetty and Emmanuel Saez, "Dividend Taxes and Corporate Behavior: Evidence From the 2003 Dividend Tax Cut," NBER Working Paper, No. 10841, Sept. 27, 2004.

James Claus and Jacob Thomas, "Equity Premia as Low as Three Percent? Evidence From Analysts' Earnings Forecasts for Domestic and International Stock Markets," *The Journal of Finance*, October 2001, Vol. LVI, No. 5.

Julie Collins and Deen Kemsley, "Capital Gains and Dividend Taxes in Firm Valuation: Evidence of Triple Taxation," *The Accounting Review*, 2000, 75.

Congress of the United States Congressional Budget Office, "How Capital Gains Tax Rates Affect Revenues: The Historical Evidence," A CBO Study, March 1988.

Dan Dhaliwal, Merle Erickson, Mary Margaret Myers, and Monica Banyi, "Are Shareholder Dividend Taxes on Corporate Retained Earnings Impounded in Equity Prices?: Additional Evidence and Analysis," June 6, 2001. SSRN: ssrn.com/abstract=272663 or DOI: 10.2139/ssrn.272663.

Dan Dhaliwal, Linda Krull, Oliver Zhen Li, and William Moser, "Dividend Taxes and the Implied Cost of Equity Capital," *Journal of Accounting Research*, December 2005, Vol. 43, No. 5, Elsevier.

Dan Dhaliwal, Merle Erickson, and Robert Trezevant, "A Test of the Theory of Tax Clienteles for Dividend Policies," *National Tax Journal*, 1999, 52.

David Dufendach, "Valuation of Closely Held Corporations: 'C' v. 'S' Differentials," *Business Valuation Review*, December 1996, Vol. 15, No. 4.

Duff & Phelps LLC, Risk Premium Report 2009, 2010, 2011, 2012, 2013.

Duff & Phelps, *2014 Valuation Handbook - Guide to Cost of Capital*, Market Results Through 2013.

Alexander Edwards and Terry Shevlin, "The Value of a Flow-Through Entity in an Integrated Corporate Tax System," *Journal of Financial Economics*, 2011, Vol. 101, Issue 2, pp. 473-491.

Merle Erickson, research published in *Capital Ideas*, Winter 2002, Vol. 3, No. 3.

Merle Erickson and Edward Maydew, "Implicit Taxes in High Dividend Yield Stocks," *Accounting Review*, 1998, 73.

Eugene F. Fama, and Kenneth R. French, "Industry Costs of Equity," *Journal of Financial Economics*, February 1997, Vol. 43, No. 2.

Foley and Lardner LLP, "More Companies Seek Alternative Means to Going Private; Out of Pocket Costs Increase by Double Digit Percentages," Aug. 2, 2007, www.foley.com/news/news_detail.aspx?newsid=3074.

Robert Frost and Michael Kenworthy, "Is There a Renewed Prospect of Going-Private Transactions?" *Piper Jaffray Middle Market Mergers and Acquisitions, M&A Monitor: Analyzing M&A Activity,* Feb. 8, 2006.

Paul A. Gompers and Andrew Metrick, "Institutional Investors and Equity Prices," *The Quarterly Journal of Economics,* Feb. 1, 2001, Vol. 116, No. 1.

David A. Guenther, "Investor Reaction to Anticipated 1997 Capital Gains Tax Rate Reduction," working paper, University of Colorado at Boulder.

David A. Guenther, "Taxes and Organizational Form: A Comparison of Corporations and Master Limited Partnerships," *The Accounting Review,* January 1992, Vol. 67, No. 1.

David A. Guenther and Richard Sansing, "The Effect of Tax-Exempt Investors on Stock Ownership and the Dividend Tax Penalty," October 2007. www.kellogg.northwestern.edu/accounting/papers/Sansing.doc.

Gustavo Grullon and Roni Michaely, "Dividends, Share Repurchases, and the Substitution Hypothesis," *The Journal of Finance,* January 2002, Vol. 57, No. 4, Papers and Proceedings of the 62nd Annual Meeting of the American Finance Association, Atlanta, August 2002.

Michelle Hanlon, James Myers, and Terry Shevlin, "Dividend Taxes and Firm Valuation: A Re-Examination," working paper, June 4, 2001, SSRN: ssrn.com/abstract=272452 or DOI: 10.2139/ssrn.272452.

Trevor Harris, Glenn Hubbard, and Deen Kemsley, "The Share Price Effects of Dividend Taxes and Tax Imputation Credits," *Journal of Public Economics,* 2001, 79.

Trevor Harris and Deen Kemsley, "Dividend Taxation in Firm Valuation: New Evidence," *Journal of Accounting Research,* 1999, 37.

Thomas E. Hartman, "The Cost of Being Public in the Era of Sarbanes-Oxley," Aug. 2, 2007, Foley and Lardner LLP.

"How to Organize Your Business," University of Maine Cooperative Extension. Bulletin #3009. www.extension.umaine.edu/onlinepubs/htmpubs/3009.htm.

IRS Databook, Table 3, "Number of Returns Filed, by Type of Return and State, Fiscal Year 2008, C Corporation Total Less Public Company Estimate Obtained," ICM Publications, www.icmasset.com/pubs/pubs_market_cap.html.

Dr. Terrance Jalbert, "Pass-Through Taxation and the Value of the Firm," *American Business Review*, June 2002, Vol. 20 (2).

Mark Lang and Douglas Shackelford, "Capitalization of Capital Gains Taxes: Evidence From Stock Price Reactions to the 1997 Rate Reduction," *Journal of Public Economics*, 2000, 76.

Jia-Wen Liang, Steven R. Matsunaga, and Dale C. Morse, "The Effect of the Expected Holding Period on the Market Reaction to a Decline in the Capital Gains Tax Rate," *Journal of the American Taxation Association*, Winter 2002.

Robert H. Litzenberger and Krishna Ramaswamy, "Dividends, Short Selling Restrictions, Tax-Induced Investor Clienteles and Market Equilibrium," *The Journal of Finance*, May 1980, Vol. 35, No. 2, Papers and Proceedings 38th Annual Meeting American Finance Association, Atlanta, Dec. 28-30, 1979, Blackwell Publishing for the American Finance Association.

Donald J. Marples, "Taxation of Hedge Fund and Private Equity Managers," *Congressional Research Service*, March 7, 2014.

Michael J. Mattson, Donald S. Shannon, and David E. Upton, "Empirical Research Concludes S Corporations Values Same as C Corporations: Part I," *Business Valuation Update*, November 2002.

Michael J. Mattson, Donald S. Shannon, and David E. Upton, "Empirical Research Concludes S Corporations Values Same as C Corporations: Part II," *Business Valuation Update*, December 2002.

Edward L. Maydew, "Empirical Tax Research in Accounting: A Discussion," *Journal of Accounting and Economics*, September 2001, Vol. 31, Nos. 1-3, Kenan-Flagler Business School, University of North Carolina, Chapel Hill, N.C.

Rajnish Mehra and Edward Prescott, "The Equity Premium in Retrospect," NBER Working Paper No. 9525, March 2003.

Rajnish Mehra and Edward Prescott, "The Equity Premium in Retrospect," *Guide of the Economics of Finance*, 2003, Elsevier, chapter 14.

Merton H. Miller, "Debt and Taxes," *Journal of Finance*, May 1977, Vol. 32, Issue 2.

Franco Modigliani and Merton H. Miller, "Corporate Income Taxes and the Cost of Capital: A Correction," *American Economic Review*, June 1963.

James Montier, *Behavioural Investing, A Practitioners Guide to Applying Behavioural Finance*, average holding period of NYSE stocks, John Wiley & Sons.

Randall Morck and Bernard Yeung, "Dividend Taxation and Corporate Governance," *Journal of Economic Perspectives*, American Economic Association, Summer 2005, Vol. 19, No. 3.

Morningstar, "Market Results for Stocks, Bonds, Bills and Inflation," *Ibbotson SBBI Valuation Yearbook*, 2009, 2010, 2011, 2012, 2013, 2014.

William Moser and Andy Puckett, "Dividend Tax Clienteles: Evidence From Tax Law Changes," January 2008.

Randi Naes and Bernt Arne Odegaard, "Liquidity and Asset Pricing: Evidence on the Role of Investor Holding Period," March 2006, Working paper 2007/11, Norges Bank, Third Annual Central Bank Microstructure Conference at the Hungarian Central Bank, the FIBE 2008, Midwestern Finance Association (MFA) 2008, European Winter Finance Summit 2008, and 2008 European Finance Association conferences and from seminar participants in Norges Bank and at the University of Stavanger.

John O'Hare, Mary Schmitt, and Judy Xanthopoulos, "Measuring the Benefit of Federal Tax Expenditures Used by Small Business," Small Business Administration, Office of Advocacy, November 2013.

John D. Phillips, "Discussion of the Effect of the Expected Holding Period on the Market Reaction to a Decline in the Capital Gains Tax Rate," *Journal of the American Taxation Association*, 2002, Vol. 24 (Supplement).

John R. Phillips, "S Corp. or C Corp.? M&A Deal Prices Look Alike," *Business Valuation Update*, March 2004.

James Poterba and Lawrence Summers, "The Economic Effects of Dividend Taxation," June 1985, NBER Working Paper No. 1353 (Also Reprint No. r0613).

Shannon P. Pratt, *Valuing a Business: The Analysis and Appraisal of Closely Held Companies*, 5th ed., New York: McGraw-Hill, 2008.

Shannon P. Pratt and Roger J. Grabowski, *Cost of Capital Applications and Examples*, 3rd ed., John Wiley & Sons Inc., 2008.

Quantria Strategies LLC, "Effective Federal Income Tax Rates Faced by Small Businesses in the United States," a study commissioned by the Small Business Administration, Office of Advocacy, Under Contract Number SCAHQ-08-Q-0012, released April 2009.

Quantria Strategies LLC, "Entity Choice and Effective Tax Rates," a study commissioned by the National Federation of Independent Businesses and the S Corporation Association, released 2013.

Craig T. Schulman, Deborah W. Thomas, Keith F. Sellers, and Duane B. Kennedy, "Effects of Tax Integration and Capital Gains Tax on Corporate Leverage," *National Tax Journal*, 1996, 49 (1): 31-54.

Jim Seida, "Evidence of Tax Clienteles for Common Stock Via the Trading Activity Following Dividend Increases," *Journal of the American Taxation Association,* March 2002.

Richard W. Sias and Laura T. Starks, "Return Autocorrelation and Institutional Investors," *Journal of Financial Economics* 46, 1997, p. 104.

United States Government Accountability Office, "Corporate Income Tax, Effective Tax Rates Can Differ Significantly From the Statutory Rate," Report to Congressional Requesters, GAO-13-520, May 2013.

"U.S. Institutional Investors Boost Ownership of U.S. Corporations to New Highs," Sept. 2, 2008, www.conference-board.org/utilities/pressdetail.cfm?press_id=3466.

Joseph Vinso, "Distributions and Entity Form: Do They Make a Difference in Value?" *Valuation Strategies*, September/October 2003.

George Zodrow, "On the 'Traditional' and 'New' Views of Dividend Taxation," *National Tax Journal,* 1991, 64.

Appendix G. Links to Selected Academic Research Papers

Benjamin C. Ayers, Bryan C. Cloyd, and John R. Robinson, "The Effect of Shareholder-Level Dividend Taxes on Stock Prices: Evidence From the Revenue Reconciliation Act of 1993," *The Accounting Review*, Vol. 77, No. 4, (October 2002). papers.ssrn.com/sol3/papers.cfm?abstract_id=324501.

Jennifer L. Blouin, Jana Smith Raedy, and Douglas A. Shackelford, "The Initial Impact of the 2003 Reduction in the Dividend Tax Rate," *National Bureau of Economic Research* (University of Pennsylvania, University of North Carolina, and NBER; www.nber.org), October 2004. papers.ssrn.com/sol3/papers.cfm?abstract_id=462542.

Jennifer L. Blouin, Jana Smith Raedy, and Douglas A. Shackelford, "Did Firms Substitute Dividends for Share Repurchases After the 2003 Reductions in Shareholder Tax Rates?" Working Paper 13601, *NBER Working Paper Series*. www.nber.org/papers/w13601.

Raj Chetty and Emmanuel Saez, "Dividend Taxes and Corporate Behavior: Evidence From the 2003 Dividend Tax Cut," NBER Working Paper No. 10841, Sept. 27, 2004. www.nber.org/papers/w10841.

Dan Dhaliwal, Linda Krull, Oliver Zhen Li, and William Moser, "Dividend Taxes and the Implied Cost of Equity Capital," *Journal of Accounting Research*, December 2005, Vol. 43, No. 5, p. 683-684. onlinelibrary.wiley.com/doi/10.1111/j.1475-679X.2005.00186.x/abstract.

David A. Guenther and Richard Sansing, "The Effect of Tax-Exempt Investors on Stock Ownership and the Dividend Tax Penalty," October 2007. www.kellogg.northwestern.edu/accounting/papers/sansing.doc.

Jia-Wen Liang, Steven R. Matsunaga, and Dale C. Morse, "The Effect of the Expected Holding Period on the Market Reaction to a Decline in the Capital Gains Tax Rate," *Journal of the American Taxation Association,* Winter 2002. aaapubs.org/doi/abs/10.2308/jata.2002.24.s-1.49.

CPSIA information can be obtained at www.ICGtesting.com
Printed in the USA
BVOW08*1602130415

395597BV00004B/4/P

9 781621 500506